WE
ARE ALL
WITCHES

First published in the UK in 2022 by
Black & White Publishing Ltd
Nautical House, 104 Commercial Street, Edinburgh, EH6 6NF

A division of Bonnier Books UK
4th Floor, Victoria House, Bloomsbury Square, London, WC1B 4DA
Owned by Bonnier Books
Sveavägen 56, Stockholm, Sweden

A CIP catalogue record for this book is available from the British Library.

ISBN: 978 1 78530 413 2

1 3 5 7 9 10 8 6 4 2

Layout by Creative Link
Printed and bound in Great Britain by Bell & Bain Ltd, Glasgow

www.blackandwhitepublishing.com

WE
ARE ALL
WITCHES

'BAD'
WOMEN
TO LIVE
YOUR
LIFE BY

MAIRI KIDD

BLACK & WHITE PUBLISHING

Mar chuimhneachan air
In memory of
Jessie Newton

'Iarram air Dia bhith riut iochdmhor
'S do leigeil am measg nan aingheal
On bha do thlachd sa cheòl san t-saoghal,
Ceòl am measg nan naomh dha d' anam.'

'I beseech God to show you mercy
And admit you amongst the angels
Since music was your delight on earth
May your soul find music among the saints.'

CONTENTS

A WHIFF OF SMOKE

THE FIRE WITHIN

TENDING THE FLAME: REMEMBERING SCOTLAND'S WITCHES

INTRODUCTION

I N EVERYTHING FROM the ingenuity of our inventors to the influence of our literature and culture, Scotland likes to think of itself as a wee country punching well above its weight, applying our particular work ethic to the betterment of the world. Unfortunately, we have also been known to bring similar zeal to less laudable aims. Legislating for the suppression of the Gaelic language might be cited as one such example, or profiting from the monumental injustice of the transatlantic slave trade. And between 1563 and 1736, we executed five times as many 'witches' per capita than anywhere else in Europe. These 'witches' were accused of using supernatural powers to cause harm to others.

In 2020 writer Zoe Venditozzi and lawyer Claire Mitchell QC launched the Witches of Scotland campaign to secure a pardon for those executed, a broader apology to acknowledge the suffering of those accused but not convicted (including those who died under interrogation), and a national memorial to support reflection and understanding of Scotland's history of witch persecution. First Minister Nicola Sturgeon issued an official apology on 8 March 2022 – International Women's Day. Meanwhile the model inspired similar campaigns in territories including Catalonia, where a pardon was issued in January 2022.

WHAT IS WITCHCRAFT?

The Scottish Witchcraft Act was passed on 4 June 1563, making 'Witchcraftis, Sorsarie and Necromancie' capital crimes. Witchcraft might be defined as the practice of magic – particularly, perhaps, malign magic – and sorcery as much the same. Necromancy has an added frisson of communication with the dead during the performance of the magical rites. But what is magic?

Magic is essentially the belief that supernatural power can be brought to bear on natural forces. In modern industrial cultures such as Scotland's, there tends to be a prevailing view that rational beliefs are what matters and magical beliefs are spurious. That doesn't stop such beliefs persisting – in 2011 the polling organisation YouGov found that around a quarter of people in the UK had consulted a psychic. A number had done so for reasons of fun or enquiry, but 14% believed that psychics could genuinely predict the future and commune with the dead.

If you're not a believer, it's easy to scoff. But you might find that even as a person who considers themselves completely rational, you harbour a subconscious belief in the supernatural. You might view an object or a place as being in some way imbued with the essence of a person, for example, so you might not wish to wear an item of clothing that belonged to a violent criminal, or conversely might wish to own an item previously owned by a celebrity. Perhaps you perform a small ritual underpinned by the idea that an action of yours could influence unrelated events, such as wearing lucky pants or squeezing your eyes shut extra hard to help a die fall on the number six. These are all examples of magical thinking and suggest that belief in magic is a fundamental property of the human mind.

The theory goes that as we evolved, we brought with us a hangover of the need always to be on the lookout for threats. Back then we were hyper alert to signs in our environment that might indicate activity by other humans or animals. Although we no longer have to worry about being eaten by a bear, perhaps we brought with us the inclination still to be on the alert for changes in our environment. And if we can rule out human or animal activity as responsible for those changes, it's a small step to see an invisible agent at play. This may underpin religious experience too.

In the early modern period, when Scotland passed its witchcraft legislation, religion was quite the hot potato. The European Reformation had seen the church split into Protestantism and what is now called Roman Catholicism. In Scotland, the Reformation Parliament of 1560 had passed the basics of Protestantism into legislation. In 1561, Mary Stuart – a devout Catholic – returned from France. Queen Mary did not assent to the Reformation Parliament's acts, but instead sought compromise until Parliament next met. This set the stage for a highly charged encounter when it convened again in 1563, but Mary had been canny. During the preceding two years she had managed to split the Protestant movement. With the support of her half-brother James, Earl of Moray, she ensured that Parliament did not commit Protestantism to legislation. They did, however, pass the Witchcraft Act.

The significant tension between the two factions in Scotland may explain the particular ferocity of the witch persecutions that followed. As the church split along the Protestant/Catholic fault line, churchmen encountered a new need to compete for believers. One way to attract them was to demonstrate effectiveness in tackling evil, for which witches were a handy cipher. Germany, the home of the Reformation, accounted for almost 40% of Europe's prosecutions. Scotland took second place.

The idea that witchcraft was automatically an evil had not always existed. The earliest texts on magic in the world are written in cuneiform script on clay tablets from ancient Mesopotamia (modern-day Iraq). These accounts of charms, incantations, exorcisms and omens speak of a society that viewed magic as part of everyday life. The tablets record no processes to discover or punish malign practitioners of magic; instead it seems that magical remedies existed to meet magical problems.

We don't know much about beliefs in the territory we now call Scotland at the same time, as the various peoples living here wouldn't get into the business of writing for thousands of years more. The earliest written record of people in Scotland comes from Classical authors and was not inclined to a positive viewpoint, given that the resistance of the 'Picti' had put an end to the Roman Empire's expansion north. But Classical accounts of Celtic-language speaking societies elsewhere, coupled with later Celtic-language texts, do support the idea that magic played a part in society. Spiritual leaders functioning also as teachers, scientists, judges and philosophers probably performed rites designed to harness supernatural power. The ghosts of these beliefs may even be spotted on the pages of early Christian manuscripts, where marvellous beasts writhe around words of scripture, and saints like Columba encounter white horses and herons, images that perhaps had special significance in pre-Christian belief.

If early Christians were open to weaving elements of older beliefs into their teachings to attract new followers, later churchmen took a dimmer view. Increasingly they defined charms, incantations and similar practice as malign witchcraft and passed laws to criminalise anyone performing them. By 1500 a new narrative had emerged in Scotland, as across Europe: the witch was in league with the Devil.

"Between 1563 and 1736, Scotland executed five times as many 'witches' per capita than anywhere else in Europe."

"The North Berwick trials – so called because the witches supposedly met the Devil in the kirkyard there – are now reckoned as the first of Scotland's five 'great witch-hunts', specific periods during which activity rose to a particular frenzy."

THE DEVIL AND THE DEEP BLUE SEA

Having defined witches as unholy and diabolical, countries active in their suppression seem to have focused on witch-hunting particularly in times of unrest and disorder or even natural disaster. In Scotland this approach was modelled by no less a personage than the king himself.

It was 1689, Mary, Queen of Scots had been dead two years and her son James was getting married. James had not yet succeeded Elizabeth I of England and was keen to develop allies for Scotland. Denmark suited both his trade aspirations and Reformed faith, and so a marriage was arranged with Anne, sister of King Christian IV. After a proxy wedding in August 1589, the plan was for Anne to travel to Scotland. She duly set sail but was driven back again and again by adverse weather conditions until the arrival of winter persuaded her to stay put. James raced north to Oslo and the couple married there. They travelled on to Denmark before returning home to Scotland in the spring of 1590.

Planning for even an averagely sized wedding can bring out the worst in people, and this one was reported to have a three-hundred-strong team working on the wedding dress alone. In Denmark, the officials responsible for conveying Anne to Scotland were accused of failing to outfit her vessel properly for the journey. They denied these charges and instead suggested that witches had sent demons to attack the fleet. A woman called Anna Koldings, already in prison for witchcraft, confessed under torture. Koldings was burned in 1590, and others she had named were accused, tried and executed.

James believed absolutely in the divine right of kings and viewed himself as God's lieutenant on Earth. Once the Danish authorities had raised the spectre of witchcraft, it was perhaps inevitable that he should decide his wedding transport woes were evidence of diabolical activity in Scotland, too. James determined to set up his own trial under the Witchcraft Act – which had seen relatively little use to date – and found his opportunity in East Lothian, where accusations were already brewing. Dozens of people would eventually be accused of using witchcraft to bring about the death of the king. James took a personal role in the process, witnessing the use of torture to extract confessions. The North Berwick trials – so called because the witches supposedly met the Devil in the kirkyard there – are now reckoned as the first of Scotland's five 'great witch-hunts', specific periods during which activity rose to a particular frenzy.

Inspired by the Danish and North Berwick trials, James wrote his 1597 book *Daemonologie, In Forme of a Dialogue, Divided into three Books: By the High and Mighty Prince, James &c.* He explains:

> The fearefull aboundinge at this time in this countrie, of these detestable slaves of the Devill, the Witches or enchanters, hath moved me (beloved reader) to dispatch in post, this following treatise of mine.

Fully endorsing the practice of witch-hunting in Protestant Christian society, the book would become a manual for British witch-finders, supplementing previous texts such as Germany's *Malleus Maleficarum* of 1486. Until the Witchcraft Act 1736 brought an end to the persecutions and instead criminalised the pretence of practising witchcraft, *Daemonologie* would play its part in all subsequent witch-hunting, including the four further major eruptions in 1597, 1628–31, 1649–50 and 1661–62.

DID PEOPLE BELIEVE IT?

On the one hand, Scottish society was one founded on belief. The official belief system certainly subscribed to the reality of witchcraft, as did the king and the authorities (naturally, since the monarchy and state were Christian institutions).

It is likely, too, that people not only read about or were told about magic by religious and political leaders, but they probably saw it in their own lives too. It is likely that unofficial magical beliefs co-existed with official religion. Divination, foretelling, charms and other rituals might have helped people deal with the myriad challenges of life, just as it might have helped them to believe that events were the will of God. Medical practice combined magical and non-magical elements, and this was true of 'official' medicine as well as folk practices. Add to that such varied factors as periods of intense personal or societal difficulty for which people sought answers, a level of social contagion and so on, and it seems quite plausible that most people did believe.

On the other hand, there are elements in certain of the witch trials that support more cynical interpretations. Let's try a thought experiment.

Your name is Janet, and you live in a small village in Fife. While you were recently away supporting your sister who was giving birth, it seems your neighbour Mary visited your house during the night. Another neighbour says she saw her leaving the house at dawn. Two days ago, you bumped into Mary and had words. Yesterday, your pig died, although previously it was in excellent health. You accuse Mary of witchcraft. What could be your motivation?

Two answers at extremes might be:

(1)   You fully believe that witchcraft is real, Mary is in league with the Devil and she has cursed your pig (it was in excellent health until yesterday, remember?)

(2)   You suspect Mary of having an affair with your husband, and the death of the pig gives you the opportunity to be rid of her. The pig was on its last legs, but no one else is to know that, and your husband is hardly likely to say anything different.

Between these extremes are all sorts of other interpretations. Your husband is as guilty as sin, perhaps, but denies having had anything to do with Mary. The only reason he can think of for what the other neighbour saw was that Mary was up to no good. Perhaps she was poisoning the pig, or worse, attempting to harm the household. You are soft-hearted and superstitious, and you believe him. Or perhaps you're prompted to make the accusation by another neighbour, or a minister, and once it's said you can hardly take it back now, can you?

This example draws from the case of Janet Wishart in Aberdeen (although Janet was not accused of cursing a pig, but rather the boys who discovered her creeping from her neighbour's house). Other examples involve individuals in authority with significant conflicts of interest accusing members of their own family or household. The types of social conflict discernible in such cases suggest a micro version of the idea that witchcraft was a handy cipher for social ills at macro level. We will only ever be able to theorise, however, why at that particular point people took so strongly to the idea that their enemies or rivals were in league with the Devil, why intense periods of persecution were followed by periods of relative inaction, and how society eventually rejected belief in diabolical witchcraft almost as completely as it had taken it up.

THE RECORD

We are not in possession of all the facts relating to witches in Scotland. Almost five hundred years of war and weather, boundary and system change, fire and pest have intervened since the passing of the Witchcraft Act. Some parts of the process were carried out locally, and local documentation is particularly vulnerable to the effects of zealous clerks, multiple removals, fire and flood. More of the central bodies' documents survive but for certain periods these are lacking, and since trial and sentence commonly became a local matter again once authorised, in the majority of cases we do not know the outcome of accusations.

Estimates of the numbers accused and the numbers executed have varied quite significantly over time. The team at the Survey of Scottish Witchcraft has worked diligently to identify the accused, and their database contains 3,837 cases,

"While not all countries focused their witch-hunting on women, women made up around 80% of the accused across Europe."

in which 3,212 of the accused are named individuals and 625 are unnamed individuals or groups. While not complete, the team considers the number to be fairly accurate. By the Survey's estimate, 84% of the accused were women.

While not all countries focused their witch-hunting on women – Iceland, for example, accused mostly men – women made up around 80% of the accused across Europe. In Scotland, *Daemonologie* made explicit the association between witchcraft and the female sex, claiming that twenty women were witches for every man. The king had an explanation for this phenomenon: 'for as that sexe is frailer th[a]n man is,' he wrote, 'so is it easier to be intrapped in these grosse snares of the Deuill . . .'

WAYWARD SISTERS?

This book focuses on the women accused in these persecutions, and on associations between women, magic and witchcraft more broadly. In doing so it does not seek to deny that men were accused too – they were, and some of their stories are referenced in these pages. But the book takes the position that witchcraft accusations in Scotland, if not quite *specific* to sex, were most definitely *related* to sex. As well as forming the great majority of the accused, women were also commonly accusers. This situation results in a rare scenario in which women come to the fore in the early modern record, and so offers an opportunity to think *around* the witch-hunts to women's broader lives.

The book is not a work of history. It is inspired by the historical record, but from that starting point it uses fiction as a means to move beyond the *persecution* of each woman featured and think instead about her *personhood*. Some stories are longer, some shorter, and you may read them together or dip in and out. In each case the book invites you, the reader, to think about your own responses to these women's stories, and what they might tell us about women in Scotland's past and present. It also sites the 'witches' in a broader landscape of women's lives, and so widens the net to include those otherwise caught up in the persecutions or characterised as witches for reasons as divergent as poetic ability or political allegiances. There are also fictional witches who remind us that Scotland had long had the concept of magical women and clung on to it – for good and ill – long after the witch-hunts ceased.

COMMON WITCHCRAFT CHARGES

PACT WITH THE DEVIL

The witch as ally of Satan was central to the early modern concept of witchcraft. Whatever the reasons for an individual coming to the attention of the authorities, when interrogated the 'witch' would be pressed to admit to having made a pact with the Devil. The purpose of body searches and 'pricking' was supposedly to find physical evidence of this pact. This was the 'Devil's mark', which was often said to have been received during a ritual mocking Christian baptism. In many cases the witch would also be encouraged to confess to having had sex with the Devil. The prominent place of this sexual relationship in interrogators' imaginations may in part explain why more women were accused than men.

ATTENDANCE AT WITCHES' MEETINGS

Any witch accused would be encouraged to confess to attendance at gatherings of witches, and to give the names of others in attendance, who could be accused in turn. Attendance at such meetings therefore might form part of initial accusations and/or of elaborations produced through the interrogation process.

DEALINGS WITH OTHER SUPERNATURAL BEINGS

'Witches' might encounter fairies, elves and the many other supernatural beings with which Scottish folklore abounds.

MALEFICIUM

The core charge against witches, the word maleficium originally meant 'wrongdoing' or 'mischief' but quickly came to be associated specifically with magical action intended to cause harm. For such a charge to be levelled it was essentially necessary only for there to have been a perceived harm. Most of these (illness, accidents) would have been the result of perfectly natural events or of chance. In some charges the witch is accused of actual assault or poisoning but generally the means employed are purely 'magical'. Maleficium commonly involved:

 Harm to humans
The theory went that witches could use their powers to bring about actual bodily harm and even death. They might do this through such means as cursing their 'victim' or looking at them in a particular way. Any illness, accident or misfortune could be ascribed to the ill will of a witch.

In some cases individuals may have experienced psychosomatic effects (physical effects deriving from a psychological condition) due to their belief in the power of witches and associated fear of harm. The intensity of peaks in witch-hunting might have encouraged such psychosomatic disorder. There is, however, no way to establish the degree to which this may have been the case. Even in the later case in Salem, Massachusetts, where there seems to have been a significant degree of 'contagion' among young female accusers, more straightforward social factors such as spite and jealousy cannot be dismissed.

 **Damage to property**

As with harm to humans, a witch might use her powers to bring about the destruction of her enemies by targeting their property, including their livestock. In this way famine, small and large-scale disasters, and the vagaries of farming in the early modern period could all be laid at the door of the witch.

 **Folk healing**

Although less common in the record than in popular imagination, folk healers (and midwives) might be accused of witchcraft for their activities. Some healers treated animals as well as people.

THE FLAMES

F WE BEGIN FROM the (hopefully) uncontroversial position that the women accused of witchcraft in Scotland did not have diabolical magical powers, because diabolical magical powers do not exist, we dismiss the possibility that those accused were accused because they were actually witches. We need, then, to ask what caused accusations to be made against particular individuals, and in particular against so many women.

We can fairly confidently state that there was prejudice against women. Society defined them as below men in the social order, the property of their fathers from birth until marriage, when they passed into the power of their husbands. King James's assertion was that they were more vulnerable to corruption as the 'frailer sex'. James is not talking about the difference in body composition that confers a strength advantage on people born male. He is talking about a propensity to superior morals and an intelligence advantage for which we know no evidence exists. Scotland sought to educate its women to a degree – the better to be good Christian mothers – but their access to education and opportunities was limited by comparison to men's. This is not, of course, an indication of lower ability.

James's belief that women were a menace in terms of witchcraft was supported by other theorists such as the author of the *Malleus Maleficarum*, who took issue both with women's weakness and with their 'insatiable carnal lusts'. It is grimly comical to read his assertion that women's higher and less regulated sex drive threatened men, given that we rather understand the male sex to be more dangerous to the female. Nonetheless, the image of the promiscuous woman persisted, in witchcraft persecutions and investigations of other 'horibill vices' such as adultery alike. There is a strong thread of prurience running through the witch trials, with many details of fornication with the Devil and other abominations of a sexual nature. One woman was even accused of causing erections in her neighbour.

Some commentators maintain that it's inappropriate to apply modern ideas of misogyny to the period in question. This appears at odds with the ways in which we view other accusations motivated by prejudice in the past. No one seriously entertains, for example, the idea that Jewish people went around poisoning wells across Europe from the late Middle Ages onwards; rather we recognise the use of anti-Semitic propaganda to justify persecution. Moreover, it would not be true to say that prejudice against women was not recognised at the time. When John Knox wrote his 1558 work *The First Blast of the Trumpet Against the Monstruous Regiment of Women,* he encountered significant resistance to his argument that women were not fit to rule. Some of this came from within his own community of Protestant reformers. John Calvin, for example, argued that there are women leaders in the Bible. When Mary I of England died – one of the women whose rule had so offended Knox – her sister Elizabeth Tudor came to the throne and barred Knox from entering England.

Elizabeth was unusual in having the power to protest. Early modern society was administered by men, for men, and few women had the power to challenge their own treatment. This is one practical reason that proportionally so many witchcraft accusations were made against women: women had less ability to challenge, especially if they were poor or unprotected. Once accused there was little a woman could say in her own defence until/if she reached court. Even there she could not speak, and so (male) connections were vital to ensure her case was made. Without these, women were more likely to be convicted and executed. This may mean that women without close male relatives were more vulnerable. But we do not know the circumstances of most of the accused on the record, and so we cannot say for certain.

In recent years a narrative has sprung up in some quarters that the accused were non-conforming, and even specifically gender non-conforming, or that they were lesbian. This does not appear to be based on fact. If it is true that the absence of male relatives rendered a woman especially vulnerable, it is not true to say that being unmarried or not the mother of sons equates to being 'non-conforming' or indeed indicates homosexuality. There were many reasons women might find themselves in such a position, much as there are today, but with the added context of high infant mortality, short life expectancy, poor healthcare and so on. Some of the accused might have been lesbian, but there is no reason to think it more likely than among the general population. In terms of gender conformity (however or whether that concept applied in the era), it seems that many charges levied at the accused were rather more based on their *conforming* to the 'frailer sex' narrative and all that went with it than not.

What this narrative may usefully do, however, is draw attention to the fact that witchcraft legislation could be used in the case of crimes (and 'crimes') relating to homosexuality. One Maud Galt, for example, was accused at the Kirk Session in Kilbarchan in 1649 of 'abusing ane of hir servants with ane pe[n]is of clay'. The authorities sought to prosecute Maud as a witch – perhaps that was easier for them to process than a lesbian sexual assault – but we have no evidence that they succeeded. It is also true that some men accused had sodomy listed among their other 'crimes'.

The accusations made against witches were to a degree generic; there was a made-up crime; the textbooks, churchmen and lawyers shaped the narrative of how it was committed; and the women could say nothing to defend themselves once accused. In the following pages you will find three women who experienced these accusations, and the worst treatment humanity had to offer.

"Faith, half the women in the country could do it if it came to a push, and if that's a crime now they'll have to arrest every howdie in the country."

TANSY AND RUE

FOR MARGERAT BANE

WHAT WE KNOW

Margerat Bane was a 'howdie', or midwife, living in Kincardine O'Neil in Aberdeenshire with clients from all social classes. She was accused of witchcraft more than once but managed to navigate the danger until 1597, when she was finally tried, as were her sister Jonet and daughter Helen. Among the charges levelled at Margerat was that she had transferred the pains of a labouring woman onto another person and killed various neighbours by such means as removing a peat from the hearth in another house and taking it to her own. Margerat's daughter Helen was accused of poisoning her daughter-in-law Bessie and bewitching the cattle and the horse of a neighbour. Both women were said to have carried out an 'erd and stane' ritual, in Helen's case in 'devilish shape'. This ritual was carried out in respect of landed property and may hint at some underlying tension relating to land boundaries or use. Margaret was tried first and executed in March 1597. She named several others who were subsequently tried. Helen was tried and executed in April.

It is commonly believed that midwives and healers were particular targets of the witch-hunters, perhaps because texts such as *Daemonologie* listed medical practice as one sign of a witch, because their work included or appeared to include magical elements, or because they were privy to intimate information and processes. Some theorists have gone further and proposed that witch-hunters were motivated by broader moves to drive women from the healing professions, clearing the way for men.

The understanding that these women were targets is supported by statements such as the *Malleus Maleficarum*'s assertion that 'No one does more harm to the Catholic faith than midwives' and by facts such as the continued inclusion into the eighteenth century of repudiation of 'witchcraft, charm or sorcery' in midwives' oaths. It is not so well supported by documentation in Scotland, however, and in the small number of cases where an accused is a midwife or healer, it is not necessarily possible to separate her profession from other factors that might have put her in harm's way.

READ ON FOR HOW IT MIGHT HAVE BEEN . . .

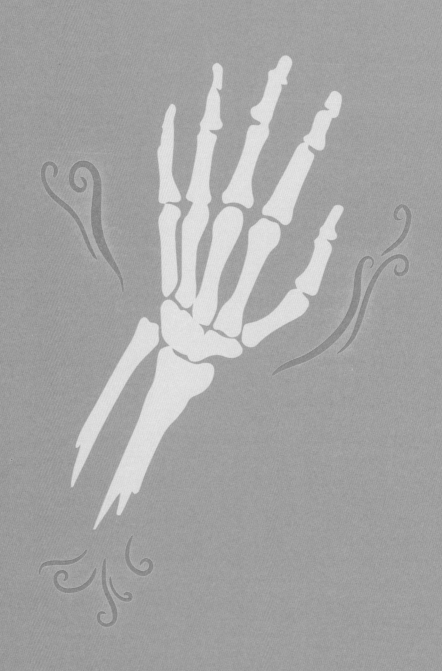

WHEN THEY COME TO question her and lay out the charges against her, Margerat is hard-pressed to understand. She's shocked, bruised, still shaken by the arrest and all that came with it, their hands rough on her as they dragged her from the house and up the brae. She had delivered one of them, laid out another's mother, coaxed three bairns from the wife of the last in safety, aye, and all three still lived and thrived, sturdy wee lads with their father's red hair and freckles. And now these men were handling her as though she were no more than an unruly cow.

She shakes her head slowly, like a child wakened from sleep, and asks them to say the charge again.

At last she understands that she stands accused of witchcraft again, this time for being able to tell when a wife was with child, and forby for helping women through the time of their travail, which is no more than any midwife would do – faith, half the women in the country could do it if it came to a push, and if that's a crime now they'll have to arrest every howdie in the country. Then they come out with some nonsense about how she was able to take the pain from some labouring woman and by some devilish means inflict it on her husband instead. The poor man fell to the ground in agony, they say, and who but the Devil could do a thing like that? Margerat snorts.

'It was drink, more like,' she says. 'Drink or squeamishness, there are many men who're happy enough getting on with their part of the business, but nine months later they turn green about the gills when the wife's end of the bargain comes.'

Would that she could give the men the pain, she thinks, though she has sense enough not to say it. She'd warrant there would be far fewer women worn out with the bearing by thirty if their guid men had to thole even half what they suffered.

They yaw on a while longer, nonsense about her taking a peat from the hearth of a neighbour to kill their child, cursing this one in the village and that, even brewing a drink that made her grandson's wife Bess sweat and burn by turns. Margerat keeps waiting for more, but the thing she most expects them to say never comes, the thing that halfway shames her, they never even blunder near it. Perhaps those to whom she rendered her service have too much of a care for their own skin to come forward and tell how Margerat Bane helped them slip a bairn.

A drink of tansy and pennyroyal and rue will do it, if it's early enough. Otherwise there are other herbs, with fearful names – black hellebore, mother of rye . . . A few grains below the tongue will save the life of a woman newly delivered when the afterbirth will not come away, and Margerat has never lost one that way yet. That's what she would tell them when they were afraid, those women who sought to rid themselves of a burden, and she would brew the awful drink with honey, for without it, it did taste of Hell itself. It was in the Bible, she would tell them, the ordeal of the bitter water in the Book of Numbers. 'And the priest shall make the woman drink the water of bitterness that causeth the curse; and the water that causeth the curse shall enter into her and become bitter . . . and then she shall be cleared, and shall conceive seed.'

Margerat left the bit out about unfaithfulness and defilement. Most of the women that came to her were not guilty of that. They weren't young girls, as you might think, but married women approaching their middle years, worn out with awful birth after awful birth, afraid that they might not survive this next one, and what would befall their children then? Some had the marks of violence on their person, an unsteady gait or a bruised face, a poorly set wrist or a strange way of turning their head since a blow had taken their hearing on one side. Others no longer had a man to keep them, they were widowed in this accident or that season of sickness. 'George Duncan will take me,' she recalls one saying, 'he always wanted me. I wouldn't go with him, for he was an auld man and I a fine girl. I'll go to him now, for what choice do I have, but he'll never take me with my belly swelling with a dead man's seed.'

She remembers every one of those women, nodded if she ever met them at market or a wedding, and saw them nod back in recognition of the secret they shared. No, none of them would have had her burn for the service she did them. It seems instead she is to be held accountable for every wee soul that came blue and strangled into her hands, every woman who died on a tide of red she could not staunch, every fever she failed to bring down – faith, even those she did, it seems, for if that sumph Bessie didn't get better after the willow bark in milk Margerat gave Helen to give her, what way was she still around to make her foolish accusations?

Margerat can see that there are those among her neighbours that cannot look on her for the memory of a bairnie lost. She knows herself the pain of losing a child, but she knows better than to apportion blame. And those women are still here to remember. There are some would say there comes a choice when things go wrong in childbed, between a mother and her child. Margerat laughs in their faces. What newborn babe can put food on the table, mend a wound its father has brought home, or soothe its brothers and sisters through a bitter season of loss?

No, Margerat knows there is no choice at all. And for all she won't say it, their foolish prattle about the Devil strikes a chord somewhere in her heart. *He* has no place at a childbed, God knows, but another has stood there by Margerat's side, often and often, one these fools would be feared to meet, though meet him they must in the fullness of time. A colder companion than the Devil, Margerat imagines, and while she has never turned to look him full in the face, she imagines that he looks with pity on the lives of men.

Perhaps she is a witch, Margerat comes to think, through the dreadful days and nights that follow. No matter what pain they inflict on her poor fingers, no matter the number of times they drag her from sleep, it seems they cannot touch the core of her at all. She is old, perhaps that's all it is, and she is done; some inner part of her is ready to meet her Maker and answer for her sins. The worst pang comes not from any mortification of her flesh, but when she understands they mean to bring her Helen here and deave her too. Helen, Margerat's summer babe, her third born but first to survive a year. Helen with the clever hands who stood so brave at her first childbed, just twelve she was then, and unpicked a whole fishing net of knots to help the bairnie come. Margerat never had any truck with any of that, but it gave them comfort, those that did believe, and Helen had the cleverest fingers you ever saw. A poppet she made for her own daughter is to be called a graven image, it seems, and it will propel her into the fire. Tears come into Margerat's eyes then, but she seals her lips. She will carry her secrets. Not to the grave – there will be no grave, she knows that; they will burn her body and scatter her ashes to the wind. She will take them with her into the fire. No word from her mouth will condemn her

Helen, and perhaps God will at last see this wrong and have an end to it.

   She has no idea what she says, of course, by the end, she is demented with tiredness and with pain. By the time they are done with her, the thing left to burn is barely Margerat at all. There is just enough of her left at the last to turn her head and open her smarting eyes. She has always known not to look until she is ready, and Lord knows she is ready now. The day is done, and he has come, as a parent might step out at sunset to lift a bairnie into bed. She has met him often enough to know that he reaches out at the last with kindness, when the pain is too much and the damage too great. She has always known he is a friend.

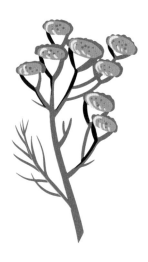

LIVE YOUR LIFE BY MARGERAT

✹ In Margerat's era, women's pain in childbirth was considered punishment for Eve's original sin, and many considered it wrong to attempt to relieve this pain. Do you see any echoes of these attitudes in the modern era?

✹ In the story (not in the historical record), Margerat performs abortions and worries that she has been arrested for it. Do you feel reproductive rights have advanced as far as you would wish in the four-hundred-plus years since Margerat died?

✹ In fiction the image of the witch as a healer, living apart from society, is quite common. Terry Pratchett's Granny Weatherwax is one example. Do you think it is reasonable to assume that early modern healers lived apart in this way? In what ways do they differ from a fictional witch?

"When they find her guilty – and they will – they will hang her by a rope of lies and they will burn her body or lay it in unhallowed ground."

DA DIM

FOR CATHEREIN THOMASDOCHTER

WHAT WE KNOW

Scotland is not culturally homogenous today, and it was even less so in the era in which the witch trials took place. The Lords of the Isles had effectively operated an independent kingdom well into the fifteenth century and the Highlands remained under clan control despite the best efforts of the Stuart monarchs to impose their version of law and order across the whole nation. Fewer witches were persecuted on clan territory than elsewhere in Scotland.

The Northern Isles of Orkney and Shetland, on the other hand, inherited a witch-hunting tradition by two separate routes. The islands had passed from Norwegian into Scottish control in the late 1400s through a marriage settlement, although Norse ownership of land continued. Both Norn and Scots were spoken and customs and laws drew from both traditions.

The witch Catherein Thomasdochter is recorded in the Survey of Scottish Witchcraft as having been resident in Foula, although the source given – *The Court Book of Shetland* – records the Catherein in Foula as being accused of theft, while a different woman was accused of witchcraft in North Yell. Catherein Thomasdochter of Yell was accused of stealing the 'profit' from milk by magical means (i.e., the fats that allow butter to be made from it).

We know nothing of either Catherein beyond these bare charges, and so this story retains Foula as Catherein's place of residence in tribute to the women accused of witchcraft whose names we have forgotten.

HOW IT MIGHT HAVE BEEN . . .

THERE IS NO COURT in this island of two hundred souls, no jail and no stronghouse. The lawman comes now and then to hear the petty crimes, the serving-lass who stands accused of stealing a few small items of linen from her mistress or the fisherman who, having lost his boat, has taken advantage of a moonless night to relieve his neighbour of a dozen saithe drying out-by in his skeo.

These matters are settled with little pain. The accused finds witnesses to speak for them, fines are paid, and then there is only the shame to bear for the guilty party, and even that fades in time. Some care little enough in the first place, of course, sunk deep as they are in drink, or so often in rough company that their crimes seem rather less a cross to bear than a fine boast to make when they are in their cups.

The greater crimes are heard in Scalloway – the murders, the grievous violences visited upon a body and the gravest of thefts. Scalloway is a grand place in Mainland, bustling with trade and travel, and crowned with a tall castle Black Patie built for himself three years back with labour stolen from every parish in the islands. There is lodging there for the accused, although none would willingly put themselves in that place.

No one in Foula has ever put their mind to what might happen if a person were to be accused of a crime of magnitude when there was no lawman due, at a time of bad weather, or when the men were busy at the harvest. Why would they? No one has anything of great value to be stolen, and no murder has been committed here in living memory, nor for many generations past.

A churchman might have known what to do in such circumstances, but there is no churchman here, in this stifling summer of 1603. The last one was carried off by a sweating sickness and no one has yet come to take his place. Perhaps there is no one to arrange it – the woman Gorvel Faderstatter, who owned Foula as part of the lands of Vaila, died last year. The island was leased to Robert Cheynes for the last thirty years of her life but King Christian far off in Copenhagen is now the owner of it all, and heaven knows he must have bigger things to worry about.

When Ingrid first hears of the thing from William, he is drunk and swollen with self-importance. These have been difficult days, with so much work stopped by the weather. There can be no fishing and precious little gleaning of birds from the cliffs, and so the men have nothing to do but watch as the bere crop is washed from the fields. Between the lightning and lashing rains it is hot and sticky, and although Johnsmas is some weeks past, still there is almost no darkness at night, so the men lie restless in their beds with want of labour to tire them out, and drift to drink to pass the weary hours.

Later Ingrid will see that this is the perfect breeding ground for thoughts of evil; as fungus grows on rye, so suspicion grows in the minds of men. Right now, though, she is busy with the baby William, and little Margret has her driven almost to distraction, apparently determined to fall heidiecra into the fire any time Ingrid's back is turned. The unseemly conduct of a lass she barely knows from the far side of the island is of little interest to her, particularly if it means listening to William puffed up with righteousness, as though he has not done his fair share of drinking, or futtering servant girls.

William has to tell her twice that the girl is to stay with them here before she hears him.

'In dis hoose?' she repeats, stupid with surprise. 'Whit wye?'

She wishes she had listened properly in the first place then, for now she must drop the kishie of peats she has carried in and listen to a repeat of William's censorious account of lewd behaviour before he explains that the choice of their home to house the witch is an honour of sorts. It shows the high regard in which he is held in the island, he says, and the fine situation of their home here, compared to the lowly state of so many others.

'An da bairns?' Ingrid asks. She has no real notion of witchcraft, and so far William's account has focused on the woman's low morals. 'Tinks du dat da witch will pit herself aboot ta hairm dem?'

William has clearly not thought of this.

'Na, na,' he says. 'Feth, it'll jöst be fower nichts, or five till dey takk her ta Scalloway.' He looks uncertain for a moment but then shakes his head, determined. 'Ee week,' he says, 'na a lok mair.'

Ingrid knows there is little profit in gainsaying him now. Whoever thought to land this burden on them read William well. They have played to the weakness of a man who inherited young, who needs to believe he has a particular standing in the place. No doubt he has agreed they will bear the cost of feeding her too.

She bends again to the peats. 'Dunna staand dere laek a deuk glyin for thunder, den,' she says. 'Midder is ben. I dinna hae time ta tell her – I hae wark ta dae. She'll be fit for tyin.'

William sets his shoulders and goes to the byre to face his mother. Ingrid allows herself a small smile. She knows the old wife will not spare him the sharp side of her tongue; he will be left in no doubt of the folly of his pride. For his part, William will revert to the habits of boyhood and the more his mother derides him, the more mulishly determined he will become.

And so it proves to be. When they come to sit to the dinner Ingrid has prepared, the old wife is as sharp as an early frost and William is slumped in a sulk. Ingrid ladles out the soup and they sup in silence. She begins to enjoy the peace and hope the whole meal may pass this way, but as William butters a second bannock the old wife hisses, 'Whaar is shö ta sleep, den? In dis hoose aside wis? Dunna be a fool, William. Shö will burn wis in wir beds.'

Ingrid thinks it's bad enough they have to house a witch; of course her mother-in-law must make an arsonist of the lass as well to add to their martyrdom.

'We'll jöst hae ta pit her i da byre, den,' says William.

'I da byre?' his mother screeches. 'Wi wir beasts?'

The old wife keeps as fine a dairy as has ever been on the island. She is harsh with the dairymaid, but softer with her cows and goats than with her family.

'Heth,' says William, 'da beasts can look efter demselves.'

'Shö will takk da profit fae da milk!' says the old wife with a shudder.

'I di hoose, den,' says William. 'On da flair.'

His mother looks like thunder, but her beasts win out over her people and she says no more.

Ingrid makes the bed up that night before they turn in. She looks at it as she smoors the fire, wondering what manner of creature will lie there tomorrow. She must have seen the lass before, but she has no real image of her. The years since she married William have passed in a blur of childbearing and rearing.

The old wife keeps to the byre the next day, and Ingrid fidgets and fusses until at last they arrive. They have brought the girl on foot, although it is many miles and the ground is so wet it is hard to tell a field from a burn in spate. It is another sullen day with thunder brewing under leaden skies; the rain has not

come but the taste of it is on the air. Ingrid stands in the door and shades her eyes to see them as they appear over the brow of the hill, one small green figure and two tall grey ones. They toil across the uthaleland and up the steep hill to the house, and at last Ingrid gets a look at the witch.

There is nothing very evil about her countenance – quite the opposite, in fact. Just a small, slight girl with blue eyes and butter-yellow hair under a neat white kerchief. Although her feet and her skirts are liberally plastered with mud, she is otherwise trimly turned out and she stands there between the two stern old men like a sunbeam between two crows.

For all her golden glow, there is a coolness about the girl, in the heat of this sticky day. Ingrid shifts her shoulders inside her own sweaty bodice, suddenly conscious of the dried milk-stains on the wool. She wishes she had taken the chance to wash. Margret hides in her skirts, uncharacteristically shy.

'Men, come awaa in,' says William. Ingrid watches as they stoop one by one under the low door. The girl stops, uncertain, and looks to Ingrid, but one of the men reaches back out and pulls her inside. William and the men sit in the chairs by the fire. The girl stands behind them.

'Will du takk a dram?' asks William. 'Or a bite o brönnie?'

Both are accepted and Ingrid busies herself fetching food and cups, hampered by Margret, who still clings to her like a limpet. Then she stands with the girl, watching the men eat and drink. Baby William begins to grizzle and Ingrid takes a seat at the back of the room to feed him. The girl watches under lowered lids, but she remains where she is.

When they have taken their fill, the men tell William they will return as soon as the weather breaks. They shake hands solemnly and take their leave, keen to be on their way before the worst of the rain. William watches them go and then it is clear he has no idea what to do next. He looks at the girl, and at his wife, and then, ridiculously, bolts out the door like a panicked colt. Ingrid can't help herself; she rolls her eyes. The girl doesn't laugh, though, and Ingrid realises she must be worn out.

'Set dee doon,' she says. 'Til da bairn has had his sook.'

The girl hesitates, then takes a seat on the stool by the wall. Margret ventures closer.

'Good day,' Catherein says to the child. 'Is du . . . William?'

Margret laughs. 'Na, Margret,' she says.

'Catherein,' Catherein tells her.

'William's my bridder,' says Margret, gesturing to the baby in Ingrid's arms.

'Ah,' says Catherein, nodding. 'Du's his peerie sister, den?'

Margret laughs at this nonsense. She seems set to go to Catherein, but just then the door darkens and the old wife comes in. Margret runs back to her mother and Catherein gets to her feet.

'Is yon da witch?' the old wife says.

Ingrid bites her tongue not to say *na, da's Queen Anne o Denmark here to see dee, Midder*. Instead she gives a curt nod. The baby is asleep now, his mouth slack. She lays him on her knee and laces up her bodice.

'Catherein,' she says. 'Catherein Thomasdochter.'

The old wife harrumphs and takes a seat by the fire. Ingrid gestures to Catherein to sit.

'Da maid has gaen hame,' the old wife announces. 'Ta keep her fae hairm.'

There is no more conversation that afternoon.

The meal that night is a sombre affair. William has been drinking and knows better than to attempt to talk, but instead sits shovelling food into his mouth as determinedly as any pig. The old wife too is silent, glowering as Ingrid takes a serving for Catherein and hands it to her where she sits on the stool. Ingrid takes her own place at the table with the others, occasionally answering Margret's prattle, but her stomach is sour and she cannot eat.

The girl rises to help clear away the food when they are done, but Ingrid gestures to her to stay where she is. After a while it seems she dozes. William sleeps too, in a chair by the fire. Ingrid and the old wife pick up mending and knitting and bend their heads to their work. Only the old wife shoots the occasional glance at the girl, as a cat might assess a swan.

When at last it is time for bed Ingrid shakes the girl awake and shows her the place on the floor where she will sleep. Then she lies beside William in the dim of the long light night and wonders how they will bear four more days of this, or five, or ten or twelve.

The next morning William and the old wife make themselves scarce, and Ingrid is left with the girl and the children again. The girl sets her bed to rights and washes out by in the rain. She eats the oatcake Ingrid gives her and drinks a cup of milk, and then she sits on the stool by the wall again where she seems content to daydream. Ingrid feeds the children, grinds meal, bakes, sweeps the floor, brings in peats for the fire. Then she goes to help with the milk, for the old wife is shorthanded without the dairymaid.

Halfway through churning the butter, Ingrid hears William set up a cry. The old wife motions for her to go, and she sets down the churn and wipes her hands, but before she reaches the door of the byre it opens and Catherein comes in with William in her arms. Ingrid's heart skips a beat, but when the girl hands her the child he seems entirely unharmed. She settles on a stool to feed him and Catherein retreats from the byre. The old wife clucks her tongue. From then on Ingrid determines that she will tie William to her back and take him with her when she goes to the byre.

Ingrid is sorry when she is done with the milk and cheese, for then she must go back into the house and be with Catherein. It rains and rains, and with the children there is no chance even to step outside. After a while she feels she cannot breathe. The girl must be unnatural, it must be true, for what person in their right mind could sit so, quiet and motionless for hours on end?

Late in the afternoon Ingrid breaks.

'Does du spin?' she asks the girl.

Catherein jumps, and Ingrid realises she was in a dwam.

'Aye,' she says. Ingrid hands her the spindle and the distaff laden with fleece.

The time passes more easily, then, for there is some company in working together. Catherein shows no great talent with the spindle and the wool she spins is rough, but it is strong and serviceable enough. When the old wife comes in and sees the two women sitting together, she shakes her head.

'My mercy,' she says, under her breath, but she makes no further fuss and, indeed, takes the baby so she may change his hippin.

Catherein helps lay the dinner out that night before she sits to eat her own. William and the old wife glower, but they say nothing and eat enough of it to suggest they have little fear of poison. Indeed, Ingrid thinks William's eye lingers a little too long on Catherein a time or two when he thinks no one is looking.

The next day Catherein brings in peats and water, sweeps the hearth and grinds the meal. She sings under her breath as she goes about her work and Margret is her shadow, until Ingrid removes the child and takes her into the byre. There Margret cries such bitter tears that the old wife gives in.

'Lat her oot,' she says. 'Afore shö spoils da cheese wi her greetin.'

Released, Margret runs back to the house. When the cheese work is done, Ingrid finds her there with Catherein. They are seated on the floor making a catch-cradle with a length of wool.

Ingrid puts William on the floor so she may go about her work. It is the first time she can remember being unencumbered by Margret since the child was born. She scarcely knows what to do with the peace, for Catherine has already baked bannocks and oatcakes and set a stew to hotter. Dried fish is soaking in milk and there is a large vessel with a lid on by the fire. Catherine opens it and smells malt.

'Ale,' Catherein says. 'Da stert o it.'

'Did dur midder learn dee yon?'

'Aye,' says Catherein. 'Shö deed last winter. My faedir soon efter.'

Ingrid feels her heart soften towards the girl. She is young to be alone in the world.

'Set dee doon,' Catherein says with a smile, and Ingrid recognises her own words of the day before. She sits and watches her daughter play with the string, her little face determined as she struggles to follow the steps Catherein has shown her. Ingrid's head nods and she dozes half an hour.

The rest does her good. Dinner is easier, her family's glares and complaints easier to bear, and that night she sleeps, some of the tension in her unwound.

But the next day the fragile ease in the household is gone. A gang of neighbours brave the incessant rain to call on the old wife, keen to steal a glance at the witch. The old wife installs herself by the fire in the oatstraw chair Ingrid brought with her on her marriage and grimly prepares to receive them.

Catherein sits quietly on her stool with her head bowed. Her eyes have a dreamy look, and Ingrid wonders where she goes when she does not wish to be here.

'Dey say shö took da profit fae da milk,' a neighbour whispers.

The old wife nods. 'I believe it,' she says, 'for has shö na taen da joy fae dis hoose? We were aa blyde afore shö cam.' She shakes her head sadly, a poor woman much put upon by her Christian duty.

Were we? thinks Ingrid wearily. She cannot ever remember there being much laughter in this house and she cannot see that Catherein has stolen any. Ingrid is baking more oatcakes, for while the neighbours have sat and steamed, they have eaten the remains

of the batch Catherein made yesterday. They come with gifts, of course – a chunk of honeycomb, a pat of butter – but they eat more than they bring.

When they are gone the old wife is in a foul humour, for she is behind in her dairying. Ingrid suggests she take Catherein to help her, but the old wife says she won't be in the same room as the witch anymore. Fine, says Ingrid, and she pulls Catherein out the door behind her to the byre, leaving the old wife with the children. The two younger women work in silence for a time, moving through the tasks together with an efficiency that belies the short time they have known one another. They are a good team.

'Whit wye does du takk da profit fae da milk?' The question is out of Ingrid's mouth before she knows it.

Catherein looks at her as though she is soft in the head.

'Dunna ask me,' she says.

Ingrid feels her face colour. 'Dey tink du did it,' she says. 'An idder tings.'

'Na, dey nivir tocht dat,' Catherein says. 'Dey taen da shance o it, ta say I wis a witch. Dae set demsels against me fir idder reasons.'

Ingrid lifts an eyebrow and Catherein sighs. 'Dere's a neebor at hame,' she says at last. 'He's had his ee on my faedir's ferm sin I wis a peerie lass. An den my faedir deed, an he cam snufflin aroond me. I said I widna hae him. But he . . . he . . . der wir some kyoderin afore I slippit him. An I . . .' She makes a vague gesture over her belly with a hand.

Ingrid puts a hand to her neck. 'Du had a bairn?' she says. 'Whaar is it?'

'It cam awa afore its time,' Catherein says. 'His midder said I kent whit ta dae ta slip it. But it jöst cam awa. An efter dat du never heard da like o whit dey fund ta say aboot me. An den dey said dey wid takk me awa.'

Ingrid sits down, her head spinning. The warp threads of this tale are the same as those in the censorious account William gave her, but now she can see how the weft has been twisted.

'Lass,' she says, 'du must tell dem he forced dee. Du wis all alane.'

'I telt dem it aa,' Catherein says. 'Dey say I must tell dem in coort in Scalloway. Den I'll get hame again.'

Ingrid feels a cold sweat break out on her back. The two scarecrows that brought the girl here knew what happened to her, William knew, and they have done nothing to help her. Worse, they have made the lies real. For Ingrid knows what will happen in Scalloway. They will speak high, confusing the girl and twisting her tale to condemn her. When they find her guilty – and they will – they will hang her by a rope of lies and they will burn her body or lay it in unhallowed ground.

Thus far Ingrid has been careful never to touch Catherein, but now she grabs the girl's wrists, hard, and shakes her. Catherein gapes at her, and Ingrid almost loses her resolve. She swallows and loosens her grip, holding to the girl as she might hold to little William.

'I dinna tink dey mean ta send dee back, Catherein,' she says, and the words make the air bitter, like ashes. 'I dinna tink . . . Dat is . . . Dey are *men*. Dey dinna seek da truth aboot idder men. Dey seek . . . Dey want . . . Dey will say du is a witch and dey must pit an end ta dee.'

'An end to me?' says Catherein. Her blue eyes cloud with confusion.

Ingrid nods. Better it come from her, now, when there might be a way to stop it. Better the girl understand the danger she is in.

'Du has cousins?' she asks, frantically trying to think of someone who will help. 'Uncles? Here, or in anidder place?'

Catherein shakes her head.

'My folk are i da kirkyard here,' she says. 'I tocht ta lie dere wi dem, my midder an my faedir.'

She begins to shake, then, and weep, and Ingrid holds her and rubs her back to soothe her as she might William. She thinks wild thoughts of finding a boat to row away, or hiding the girl in a cave or some other dark place in the island. For a desperate moment she wonders if the two of them should jump from the cliffs – a moment's flight, and it would be a quick end. But just then Margret creeps into the byre to find them and Ingrid is ashamed. Catherein wipes her eyes on her apron and holds her arms out for the child. Margret clambers onto her lap.

That night Ingrid seats Catherein at the table. She expects William and the old wife to protest, almost welcomes the promise of a fight, but they seem to recognise that something has changed in her. They barely meet her eye, but meekly eat and drink what they are given.

The next day Catherein is sick, her skin pale and clammy. Ingrid puts her into her own bed and tells William he can sleep in the byre. She expects dissension but none is forthcoming. William seems heartily sick of the business.

When her work is done, Ingrid clambers in beside Catherein and the girl turns into her arms. She feels tiny and frail in Ingrid's embrace, barely bigger than a child.

The next day Catherein is a little better. Margret climbs into the bed with her string and demands a game of catch-cradle. Then she begs to be allowed to use Ingrid's comb, her most treasured possession. Ingrid gives it to her and Margret spreads Catherein's hair out on the pillow and combs it through, again and again. Catherein lies with her eyes closed and does not protest, although the child is not the gentlest.

Ingrid sticks her head out the door every hour, hoping for rain, but it does not come. The terrible closeness is gone. The weather has broken at last.

That night William sleeps in the byre again. Margret gets into bed with her mother and Catherein. She kicks and twists as children do, and Ingrid gets up to put her back in her own bed. Catherein puts out a hand to stop her.

'Lat her be,' she whispers.

The next afternoon the men arrive. This time there are more of them, and they come by boat, ready to take Catherein across the sea. Margret cries and cries and will not be wheeshed. While a grey-faced William talks to the men, Ingrid wraps a bundle with food and jars of ale, a blanket and a spare shift. At the last minute, she tucks in her precious comb.

Catherein sits on the stool until it is time to leave. She is pale, still, and she seems less dreamy than she was, and more exhausted. When the men motion for her to come, she hugs Margret and bobs a curtsey to Ingrid. Ingrid gives her the bundle and places a hand briefly on her head. Catherein looks up into her eyes.

They stand at the door – Ingrid, William and Margret – and watch the small procession as it picks its way down to the shore. The men lift Catherein into the boat and hand her bundle in after. As they row out into the stream, Catherein turns back. Ingrid watches her white face until they are gone. William takes Margret inside then, but Ingrid stands a few moments longer, her face wet, before she turns to follow. She starts when she sees the old wife in the door of the byre, looking to sea. They exchange a long look Ingrid cannot read. At last she turns and walks into the house.

In a few weeks' time news comes that the witch Catherein Thomasdochter has been put to death.

The season that follows is a blighted one for the farm.

The rains return at harvest time. A third of the crop is ruined. It will be a hungry winter.

The cow takes an infection in her udder and her milk is streaked with blood.

The old wife is taken ill, a strange weakness come over her one evening. They take her to bed and she seems to sleep, but in the morning she cannot move her right side. Her face is strangely contorted, one eye fallen somehow and her mouth twisted and useless. She lingers for several weeks in bed, and then slips away in her sleep.

If a person knew no better, they might say that the place was bewitched, but at least some in Foula have learned never to risk such words again.

William drinks more and more. Sometimes in the night Ingrid hears him weeping. At first the anger is so great that she cannot bring herself to comfort him, but eventually she softens. He turns to her like a lost child.

The days shorten. The darkness is a blessing, for there is time to grieve.

LIVE YOUR LIFE BY CATHEREIN

★ The theft of 'profit' or 'goodness' from milk is a crime witches were commonly accused of, especially in folk lore. Do you think other reasons might exist for issues in milk yield or quality in cattle (or indeed any mammal)?

★ One theory for the stop-start pattern of witch-hunting, in which intense periods of activity were followed by long lulls, is that witch fever rose in pitch when society faced particular disruption. Do you think there may be a link between 'dairy' witchcraft accusations and difficulties facing communities?

★ In the fictional version of Catherein's story in this book, Ingrid initially believes that Catherein is guilty of 'dairy' magic but comes to see she has done nothing wrong. Do you think it is likely that some people saw the injustice of the accusations? If they did, why would they not speak out?

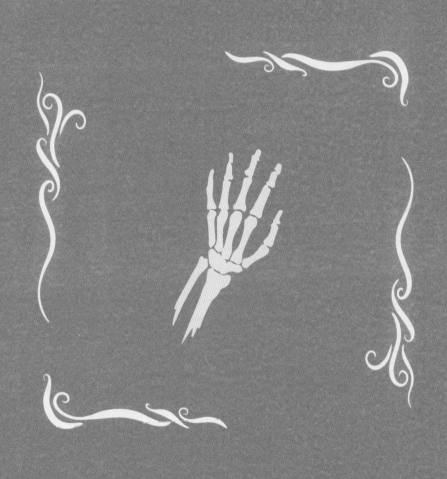

"How can they have expected you to understand the world should have no magic in it? It's in your bones, the knowledge, taken in as if with your mother's milk as it formed them."

SORROW AND SIGH AND MEIKLE CARE

FOR ISOBEL GOWDIE

WHAT WE KNOW

I sobel Gowdie's is perhaps the most infamous Scottish witchcraft case, due in part to a series of four lurid confessions Isobel made in 1662 without, or so the record claims, 'violent torture'. Before the local landlord, minister and other assorted lawmen, Isobel testified to a sexual encounter with Satan, to turning herself into a hare, to involvement in the deaths of one of her interrogators' children, and more. We cannot state with confidence why she did so. She might have been led by her interrogators, or terrorised into repeating details of cases she had heard elsewhere. She might have been suffering from dementia or mental illness. She might have been a wild fantasist, or inadvertently or otherwise have consumed hallucinogens. She may have been deprived of sleep as we know other accused witches were. Today sleep deprivation as an interrogation technique is prohibited by international law as torture or ill-treatment. It quickly causes disordered thoughts and irrationality, followed by a continuing decline in cognitive function. The subject will eventually hallucinate and experience a break with reality.

The sexual detail Isobel ventured in her confessions is startling – such as the Devil's semen being the temperature of spring water – and she was not alone in volunteering such. Society at the time centred sex in discussion of sin, and gossip about sexual 'deviance' may have informed confessions. Other theories include the possibility that by employing what effectively amounted to sexual abuse – stripping and intimate body searches – they provoked already traumatised and confused women into reliving past sexual experiences, including any assaults they had suffered.

Despite the infamy of Isobel's case, we do not know many of the facts of her life such as her date or place of birth, her parentage or whether she ever had any children. At the time she was accused she was living with her husband John Gilbert by Loch Loy in the parish of Auldearn near Nairn, where John worked the land. Nairn itself was a community in cultural transition, still retaining an older community of Gaelic speakers alongside newer Scots and English-speaking neighbours. There may have been tensions between these communities, or not. We don't know why Isobel was accused, and we don't know what ultimately happened to her. She was most likely tried and executed, but no records survive.

HOW IT MIGHT HAVE BEEN . . . .

HOW CAN THEY HAVE expected you to understand the world should have no magic in it? When your first memory of anything much at all is the night you first saw angels in the sky, huddled in your father's arms as they leaped across the dark, green and pink and gold, the Merry Dancers?

When you've lived your whole life with perfect care so that you might never attract the attention of the other ones, the little folk that fell from Heaven and made their homes in the dark, hidden places of the earth? Passing with quick steps by the hillock where an unwary maid dallied long ago, never to be seen again but only heard, so they say, on a winter's night, when a drunk man might pass that way and swear he heard a woman's voice lamenting. On the night of a wedding, a ring of pins around the sleeping cows would see you return to milk in the forenoon, and a piece of iron in a child's cradle was a charm all mothers knew against finding that same cradle empty one awful morning.

It's in your bones, the knowledge, taken in as if with your mother's milk as it formed them. The falling sickness is cured by a draught of water from the skull of a suicide. A child that is bonny and blithe one day and withers and sickens the next cannot be cured, for it is a changeling and the fairies will never return the real babe once they have it. If a man's gums bleed and you find blue spots on his shins, cut an apple into four, bless each piece with the name of the Trinity and have him eat them up.

They don't want to know about that last one, Park the Laird and the others; prayers are of no use to them. Not what you say when you rise in the morning or smoor the fire at night, half-remembered blessings you heard from your Granny. She had Gaelic, Father's mother, and you have none but for a few half-words here and there.

They tell you that you're lucky, Park and his cronies, for they have laid never a hand on you in all the time they have held you. Witches in other parts have their foot bones broken, they say, or their fingernails drawn out with pincers. In

England, Forbes tells you, they swim them, both thumbs tied to their great toes with a cord. Water is too pure for the vile body of a witch, he says, and if she is guilty it rejects her. His long white nostrils twitch so you're hard pressed not to smile; it's long been said in these parts that the minister likes women little enough, and if you must send your lad to him on an errand, best advise he keeps his back against the wall. Laughter bubbles up like water through a spring until it chokes you.

That turns you to think of some poor old crone, bound and floundering in mud and weed, and you feel you could look her in the eye without shame, for it seems to you that you understand what it is to sink into the deep, only to be dragged back up into the light and thrown gasping on the ground with the taste of death in your mouth. It's been days since they let you sleep, and now, when you nod and they jab you, your wame lurches so you fear you'll void your dinner on the floor. Still they jabber on, Dallas and that Dunbar, with tales of pincers and branks, and pins to find the secret places the Devil has suckled you.

You have no idea how long they've had you when your mouth opens of its own accord and you tell them you met the Devil in the kirkyard of Auldearn – damn that whoreson Forbes with his fondling of children, may the stink cling to his precious kirk like shite – and renounced your baptism. You close your eyes and think of that crone bound and choking in a far-off country and tell them you touched your foot and your thumb to your head and it was your shoulder He suckled, for you're damned if you'll give these clarty-minded bastards the chance to fumble between your legs; you've seen the swelling in Dunbar's breeches as he eyes you.

Now you've begun you cannot stop. You tell them you fucked your Master in the keep at Inshloch and how you and Janet Breadhead raised a child from its grave and some nonsense about ploughing with puddocks. And then you see that bastard Park, who levies rents that take the bread from children's mouths, and his eyes are shining; this is what he wants. And you find a shard of ice somewhere in your heart and hold to it, and then you are telling the fucker that it was you that killed his children, all those little corpses he sired, it was you and Janet and Margaret Wilson.

And then the names pour out of you, names and more names, so he will never again sleep easy in his bed with the knowledge that half his tenantry hate him with such cold and bitter hatred that they would take his very children from him. And you know you shouldn't do it, your words will shake your neighbours from their warm cot-houses and into the fire, but you can see it in his eyes, the terror and the grief, and you know he will never again rest in a room where the door is not bolted.

And so for good measure you tell him you can turn into a bird at will, a black one, a mocking, jeering jackdaw that stands on the ruins of a man and laughs. And there is more, how you can make the blackest dyes in the Devil's vat, and God it is true, your heart is black now; if they pierced it, the blood would flow out thick and dark and drown them all in their dirt.

It is written down and then – there is sleep.

LIVE YOUR LIFE BY ISOBEL

★ Beyond the basic fact that Isobel was a woman, do you think her case supports or challenges the claim that witchcraft accusations were related to sex (as in, the female sex)?

★ What effect might it have had that Isobel was interrogated only by men, and these were rich or learned men while she was (most likely) minimally educated and relatively poor?

★ Isobel named other women as her accomplices. She may have been socialised to believe women were more likely to be witches. Do you recognise the characterisation of some women working against other women's interest in patriarchal societies?

BETWEEN THE FRYING PAN AND THE FIRE

WHILE WOMEN MADE up the great majority of accused witches, those who carried out the justicial process were almost exclusively men. The different prosecutions involved combinations of local churches and their courts, local sheriff and burgh courts, the court of justiciary in Edinburgh and its travelling circuit courts, and central structures such as the privy council and parliament, which in turn gave authority to hold yet more local courts. All of these were structures created and administered by men.

This is not to say that women played no other role in the process than to be the victim of it. Witches could be convicted on several types of evidence:

* Their own confessions, obtained in many cases under torture
* The testimony of others in the community, usually detailing the harm done to the individual by the witch
* The testimony of other witches, again obtained in many cases under torture
* Physical evidence on the body of the witch in the form of 'the Devil's mark'

Women were not involved in carrying out interrogations. They were, however, involved in giving and procuring all of the other forms of evidence in this list.

Women commonly testified against other women, because it was common for accusations against witches to originate with other women. Why was this the case?

The context for accusations was not neutral. For one thing, women had more to do with other women than they did with men. Even today it is common for women to have more female friendships and men more male; in the early modern era there were strong concerns around interaction between the sexes to contend with too, and women tended to be more confined to the private sphere. More social interactions with other women meant more chance of quarrels and other tensions with other women, and so more meat for accusations. Added to this, women may have been loath to accuse men, since men had more power.

Women were not a homogenous group then as they are not now, and their motives for making accusations will have varied. Undoubtedly some will have fully subscribed to the belief that witches were hateful and dangerous and should be eradicated, and within this group some would have fully subscribed to the belief that women were defective creatures when it came to ability to resist the Devil and his wiles, and therefore more likely to be witches. Even those who might have thought to question these orthodoxies are likely to have internalised the narrative to some degree. It is natural for people to look for 'answers' in the aftermath of an unexpected loss, death, accident or illness, and in the time period in question many events we understand today would have seemed explicable only through a religious or magical narrative. It is also natural for women living in strongly patriarchal societies to internalise messages about the inherent inferiority of women. Even those who might have made an accusation maliciously were using these structures against their own sex. Given the fact that periods of intense accusation tended to focus on one local area, some might even have seen the writing on the wall and thought, 'better her than me.'

The question of why accused women accused other women under interrogation is rather simpler; they did so for the same reasons they made the rest of their 'confessions'. Tortured 'violently' or through such means as sleep deprivation, threatened, humiliated and bamboozled, many eventually gave the authorities what they wanted. Even in extremis, however, some managed to outwit their interrogators. Before she died during the period of her interrogation, Fife woman Lilias Adie named 'accomplices' who had already been accused or were already dead, thereby cheating the executioner of more women for his flames.

Discovery of the Devil's mark was another area in which women were less active. This 'investigation' was based on the belief that the Devil left a sign on his followers' bodies to mark their pact with him, in a mockery of Christian baptism. The mark was variously understood as a visible blemish or a spot on the body insensitive to pain. Whichever form it took, discovery of the mark necessitated stripping the accused and often shaving their hair. They were then either inspected – the mark was often 'found' in their private parts – or jabbed all over with a stout pin or an awl until a place was found that did not bleed or pain the accused. Sexual assault was thereby added to the list of tortures employed.

In many cases 'witch pricking' was done by the interrogators themselves but on occasion they had the support of a professional witch pricker. Around ten of these individuals were known to have operated in Scotland. It was a role for men, but one infamous woman practised while dressed as a man.

In the following pages you will find three women whose very different actions facilitated the charging and execution of other women.

"What form do you believe the Devil takes? Some say he is a great beast – others maintain he has no body to speak of at all; rather his evil is in the air, bellowing like thunder, or whispering sweet inducements in a woman's ear."

BINDINGS

FOR GEILLIS DUNCAN

WHAT WE KNOW

Gelie or Geillis Duncan's name is perhaps more famous now than it has ever been in the four-hundred-plus years since she died. This is thanks to the *Outlander* novels by American author Diana Gabaldon, and their successful television adaptation. Gabaldon plays fast and loose with Scottish history, culture and language, not least in her portrayal in the first book of the series of a witch trial. This process is conducted under the nose of a clan chieftain by some form of travelling ecclesiastical court that didn't exist in Scotland, around twenty years after the last witch trial was held here, and when legislation no longer permitted the trials. Unlike in the real-life persecutions there's an actual witch involved, who also happens to be a murderess, a sensualist who likes to dance naked outside at night and an all-round problematic person. It might be charitable to acknowledge that the Geillis character is also a time-traveller from the future and Gabaldon might say she chose the name for herself in tribute to the real-life 'witch'. It does seem a shame, though, to disregard the fact that the real Gelie was no witch at all, but rather a (probably teenage) victim of judicial torture and murder.

The real Gelie was a servant in the house of David Seton in Tranent. Seaton was bailie depute and a person of some standing locally. He first accused Gelie of witchcraft on the basis that she was out a lot at night. The pamphlet *Newes from Scotland* also explains that Gelie *'took in hand to help all such as were troubled or greeued with any kinde of sicknes or infirmitie: and in short space did perfourme manye matter most miraculous.'*

Gelie's thanks for this useful service was to be imprisoned by Seton and his son (also David Seton). They had no authorisation to do so, although it seems no one was censured for this. They and their associates subjected Gelie to pilliwinks – a device to compress the thumbs – and 'thrawed' her with a rope tightened around her head. She was also searched for the Devil's mark. Unsurprisingly, Gelie confessed, and named multiple accomplices. She maintained that she had done little magic herself, however, aside from bewitching a hat. But matters were to escalate. The king was home from honeymoon and taking an interest in witchcraft. What had begun with the Setons would bloom into a process affecting dozens of people from all levels of society, from the Earl of Bothwell to local schoolmaster Dr Fian (aka John Cunninghame) to poor Gelie.

Among the women Gelie named as witches were two high status individuals, Barbara Naper or Napier and Euphame MacCalzean. Euphame was the daughter of Lord Cliftonhall, and had inherited his considerable property on his death. She was married to the brother of David Seton's wife, but not happily. When Euphame was convicted, her property was seized for the king, but once she had been burned it was returned into the control of the males of the family. Since Euphame had only daughters, Seton's brother-in-law gained significantly from this turn of events. Before Gelie died she retracted her accusations against MacCalzean and Naper, saying these were forced. This may have supported Seton et al in making the case for the return of Euphame's property.

When King James heard in another confession that Gelie played the Iewes (Jews') Trump for the witches, he requested that she be brought from prison to play for him. She is the first person in Britain recorded as playing the instrument, and (thankfully) the only one recorded as doing so with hands injured through torture. A later illustration shows the encounter. Gelie appears as an old woman, although in truth she was probably quite young, perhaps even in her teens.

Gelie was executed on 4 December 1591 at the Castle Hill in Edinburgh. She was strangled before her body was burned.

HOW IT MIGHT HAVE BEEN . . .

THEY COME WITH THEIR thumbscrews and pincers, their hammers and heated iron to force a confession from her lips. In faith they need them not, for is it not true, the thing they desire her to say? Geillis Duncan does serve a dark master.

What form do you believe the Devil takes? Some say he is a great beast – half man, half bull it seems, or like a dog, or a giant black dragon. Others have it that he can take the form of anything at all – a hayrick, perhaps, or a stack of logs. Others maintain he has no body to speak of at all; rather his evil is in the air, bellowing like thunder, or whispering sweet inducements in a woman's ear.

In some tales Satan appears simply as a man. This Devil comes to a married wife in the guise of a love long-lost. Seven years is nothing, he tells her, the blink of an eye, and if she will leave her guid man and baby child, they may travel the seas together and see the lilies grow on the banks of Italy. She holds out for a time, the goodwife, professing her love for her husband, her commitment to her marriage vows and so on. Then the lover offers her riches beyond her wildest dreams and off she sails on the greatest of his seven ships, where three leagues from shore she will notice the cloven hooves that hide below his breeks. Too late, mistress, too late. The bright hills of Heaven will never be yours; a watery end awaits you.

This last Devil is most like the one that Geillis knows, but there is one difference. In the songs, the stories, the Devil must have the assent of the woman he woos before he may take her. As long as she refuses, he cannot abduct her.

When Geillis's master first came to her there was no asking. She woke in the deep of the night to find him in her room, Maggie being dispatched on some errand designed to get her out for half an hour. At first Geillis did not understand, stupid with tiredness and doubly so with youth, as he ordered her to bend over the bed and lift her shift. A beating was what she expected, and she was wracking her brains to work out which mistake of all she had made that day had occasioned it, when it became clear that he intended something else entirely.

When he was done he told her to clean up the mess, and she did so as quickly as she could, her hands shaking as she stuffed the rag into the fire and raked the cinders over it lest Maggie should come back and understand what had happened. When at last Maggie stumbled in, cold and lumbering with exhaustion, Geillis was in bed with her eyes tight shut, feigning sleep that would not come.

There were no seven ships for Geillis, of course, no lilies, but there were some small changes to her situation. The master was a fastidious man, always clean of collar and cuff and scented with the lavender they laid between the starched garments in the kist in wash week. He was alert to unpleasant odours, and after a few nocturnal visits to Geillis's room he commented loudly to the mistress while they sat to their meat that the smell of the servants was troubling to him. And so the mistress decreed that Maggie and Geillis should wash more often and have more changes of linen. That meant more clothes come wash day and more fetching of water, of course, but there was a small reward in that they were given herbs for their washing bowl, soft cloths, and even the last slivers of the mistress's fine soap from Spain.

Maggie cared more for sleep than castill soap or camomile water, and she rubbed herself clean as roughly as ever on the way to or from her bed, thinking only of the fastest route to oblivion. Geillis slept increasingly badly, and she found the ritual of the soap and the scented water a comfort. As she steeped, lathered, wiped, washed, her breathing calmed and her mind cleared. Her memory was rinsed clear with her hands; like a babe raised from the baptismal font, she was clean and new.

But as the weeks became months and the master's visits continued, Geillis found it harder and harder to keep herself clean. No matter how she scrubbed in the morning, she would catch a whiff of rot on her skin by noon. In turn the foulness loosed a wheel in her brain that spun memories and thoughts around and around unsought, so that she started when the master came into the room or froze at the sound of his voice. She was right in the middle of the floor, one day, carrying a dish of peas to the board for shelling, and Maggie ran right into her where she had stopped dead, breaking the dish and scattering the peas into the rushes of the floor. Geillis earned a clout across the lug for that from the master and then a strapping from the mistress with the master's heavy leather belt. They were both in a foul temper that day, some business with the mistress's goodsister MacCalzean had enraged them, and Geillis was beaten half to death before the mistress was done. The master watched.

The master and mistress took themselves off

then to meet her brother Patrick at another brother's house where they could complain of Patrick's wife, and Maggie helped Geillis limp back to their room. She cleaned the weals on Geillis's legs with a cloth soaked in vinegar – briskly, for she had the work of two to do now and no wish to earn a beating of her own – and then she scurried back to the kitchen. Alone in the quiet, Geillis poured water into the basin and scrubbed and scrubbed at her hands, her arms, between her legs. At last, when she too had drawn blood, she was shriven.

Geillis's legs healed over the next while, but her hands grew worse and worse. They never had been soft, the lye and the laundry had seen to that, but now they became angry and scaly, the knuckles cracked and bleeding, the webs between the fingers blistered and weeping. At the kirk she sat on them to hide them, but she knew that others saw.

'The oil from sheep's wool,' an older woman said to her in passing one Sabbath. 'It will soothe your hands. Come and see me and I will make you a salve.'

Geillis began to say that she had no money – the master held their wages, for safe-keeping he said – but the woman cut her off. No need for payment, she said, or payment in kind would do, for she had work enough for two and only herself to do it.

The next time the master and mistress were from home Geillis went to the house the old wife had told her. This was not her own home – that was some six miles off, in the hills at Nether Keith – but the home of a daughter of hers where she stayed for convenience when she was attending a birth or a sickbed. Her name was Agnes and she was a well-known healer; many women sought her out when they were near their time.

On that first visit Agnes was as good as her word. She drew Geillis's hands to her and dipped her fingers in a pot of salve that smelled of sheep and summer. This she worked into Geillis's poor hands and then she wrapped them in soft rags and bound them up.

'Leave them so for tonight,' she said, 'and if you can keep them bound up tomorrow too, so much the better. Come back the next night and I will see how they fare.'

Geillis asked then what she could do in payment, for Agnes had mentioned work. But Agnes said she must heal Geillis's hands first, before Geillis could be of use to herself or anyone else. She said that Geillis could sit by her and keep her company while she pounded a salve and prepared a poultice. Her daughter was worn out with caring for her babes and had already gone to her bed. Agnes needed little sleep – the old often do not, she said – and the long nights were lonely for a widow woman.

Geillis sat, then, with her bandaged hands and a glass of hot wine while Agnes worked, and answered all the older woman's questions about herself and her family and her master and mistress. Agnes knew of the master, of course; there were few in the county who did not know of Bailie Seaton. She asked Geillis what manner of man he was.

Geillis's tongue froze then, and she began to pluck at the bandages on her hands.

'Leave off that,' Agnes said, taking the bandaged hands between her own and holding them still. She sighed then, and trapped both Geillis's hands in one of her own. With the other she added a tot of something from a jug into Geillis's cup and pushed it towards her.

'Drink up,' she said. 'And tell me all, lass. I'm hard to shock, and better you tell it to me than you keep taking it out on your poor hands.'

The liquid in the cup was fiery and Geillis choked on it. When she had control of her voice again, she stuttered out an account of the master's visits.

'Bastard,' said Agnes, when she was done. She poured another tot of the liquid into Geillis's cup and Geillis drank it. She was beginning to feel warm and heavy now, and almost as though some part of her was floating. She heard a giggle from her own mouth, followed by a hiccup.

'You'll stay here tonight, lass,' Agnes said. 'You can sleep on my blankets by the fire and I'll sleep in the chair. In the morning we'll see what's to do about all this.'

Geillis slept without dreaming and woke to the bustle of children and breakfast. When they had supped Agnes walked her home to the Setons', carrying a basket of cures for the various folk she was to visit that day.

'Mind what I said about your hands, Gelie,' she said. 'Keep them bound up and come back to my daughter's house tomorrow after dark. I begin to see a way to keep you out of harm's way, but I need to think on it some more.'

Geillis was able to follow these instructions with the mistress's blessing, for when she saw the bindings she nodded and said she was relieved, for Geillis's hands had been putting the master off his meat. She was in a state of high

agitation, the mistress, for it transpired that her brother Patrick had gone off to France, leaving his wife in charge of all their business. This was the goodsister the mistress hated, the woman MacCalzean, who had kept her own name on marriage and controlled the fortune she had inherited from her father for all that she was nothing but his bastard daughter. It seemed to affront the mistress, that, and to add insult to injury the mistress believed that this woman had somehow tricked the mistress's own father into leaving her and her husband a far greater share of his estate than they deserved, so that the mistress and her family missed out, who had so much less to begin with.

So much Geillis and Maggie heard, for a confidante of the mistress was visiting and in their indignation they neither of them could keep their voices down. Geillis filed it all away in her mind and told it to Agnes when she returned to see her the following evening. Agnes pronounced herself well pleased with Geillis's hands when she had stripped them, and she applied more of the salve and bound them again and made her promise to leave them be another two days so the skin could heal. Geillis promised, but even as she spoke her fingers worried at the knots. Agnes saw, and she drew Geillis over to a seat by the fire.

'I want you to do this thing not for you, or your mistress,' she said, 'but for me. I want a lass, see, to help me in my work. My eldest daughter has no time for it, as you can see, and my next eldest is at home minding the younger ones. I can train you up, Gelie, as my folk trained me, and then you may have a chance to leave that house and live as your own woman. And until then, you must sleep under his roof as little as you can manage. Stay there when they are from home or there are guests in the house, for he is no danger to you then. Otherwise, come here to Helen's house and she will give you a bed whether I am here or no.'

Agnes said this last with a triumphant smile on her face and for a moment Geillis's heart lifted, but she knew she could not accept. Agnes's face fell as she stammered out her thanks, and her refusal.

'But why, lass?' she said. 'Why ever no?'

'Maggie,' Geillis said simply. 'He would just turn to her. What is my safety worth if it is at the price of hers?'

Agnes had no answer to this, but her daughter Helen chipped in.

'I dinna think he will go after Maggie,' she said. 'Her father's house is ten minutes' run across the fields, her mother still living. She sits with them in the kirk on Sundays, Gelie, and they are well liked hereabout. Far too much chance she would tell.'

'True,' Agnes said. 'And did you not say he makes sure to get her clear before he gets his filthy thing out with you?'

Soon it was decided; Maggie was safe and to make doubly sure, Helen would have a word with her mother to ensure she would keep an eye on things.

It worked well, their solution, for while Geillis expected to meet objections to her staying away at night, the mistress was tight with her coin and any small saving of firewood and rushlight, food and ale was a welcome one. Geillis ate her evening meal at Helen's often, taking mending and ironing along in a basket. Helen helped with it, admiring the fine clothes and even trying them on now and again. Geillis helped Agnes to pound her salves and steep her tinctures. She learned the herbs that would start a labour or heal a wound, plasters that would clear congestion in the chest and gargles that would salve pustules in the throat. Agnes took her to births and sickbeds, taught her to clear a newborn's nose and lay out a corpse.

Agnes was a thinker, fascinated by the things she did not know. Although she did not read well, she had a friend who was a schoolmaster nearby at Prestonpans and he read the latest herbals and works of anatomy and told her what they contained. He was a peculiar man, this Dr Cunninghame, fascinated by the mind and its workings. He believed that the mind could heal the body and that it was possible to put people into something like a waking sleep where they would be freed from fear and restraint. He wanted Agnes to try this on one of her birthing women to help with the pain, but Agnes drew a line at that, telling him she had no truck with such beliefs.

'"That's rich when you have your loosening of knots and mumbling of prayers," he says to me!' Agnes told Geillis. 'I says, "But that's just to keep them from fretting." And he says, "Aye Agnes, and that's what I'm telling you, do away with the fretting and you might do away with the pain!" And then he told me he had brewed a drink from mushrooms that would take them out of their earthly bodies so they would not suffer so much, they did it in heathen times. And – wait till you hear this – he says that pins pricked into certain parts of the body can soothe pain or distemper in the other parts! The man's a fool.'

Geillis quite liked the sound of the drink but she did not say so. In fact, she almost felt that she had escaped from her own earthly existence, so complete was the relief at her freedom from the master. There was still laundry to do at the Setons', water to fetch, food to cook, pots to empty and all the rest of the endless labour of the household, but while she did it she could think of more interesting things. Maggie seemed quite herself, every bit as placid and lumbering as before. Her work finished before Geillis's, of course, because now she also worked for Agnes, but that did not tire her, rather it lifted her up. Now she had a skill, others trusted her, and she could be of use to more than the Setons. Maggie burned her hand and Geillis made a salve and bound it so that it barely scarred. The neighbours' lad James took a raging sore throat that gave him such fever he looked like to die, but Geillis nursed him through. Soon the good folk of Tranent had come to look on Geillis as a healer in their midst, and to call on her when they had need.

Busy with household and healing, Geillis had ceased to think of the master much at all. She thought of him so little that it never crossed her mind to wonder whether he still thought of her. But think of her he did; in fact, he thought of her often, furious that a man such as he could be outwitted by a girl of sixteen, a maid in his house.

Things were not going well for David Seton. There had been money problems for some time, and now these problems had become severe. Keen to show a lifestyle in keeping with their station in the town, the Setons had extended themselves too far. All would have been well, had Katherine received the portion of her parents' estate she expected, but of course her scheming brother Patrick and his wife took almost all of it. Had Patrick Moscrop been a stronger man he might have prevailed upon the bitch MacCalzean to do something for the Setons, but he was terrified of the woman, endlessly bleating that she was trying to poison him. Seton couldn't see why she would bother; the woman had faced down stronger adversaries in her time. Now Patrick Moscrop was off to France and Seton could not countenance the thought of going to MacCalzean on his knees to beg for relief. He gnawed away at the problem endlessly, the black thoughts taking over his every waking minute. And then he began to see a way he might outwit Euphame MacCalzean, and punish the serving chit for good measure.

The morning they took her, Geillis had spent the night with Agnes and Helen. For once there was no birth to attend and no sickbed to stand over,

and as it was coming on for winter Agnes had most of
her herbs put by. The bairns were asleep, Agnes
had a bottle of bramble wine she had been given in
payment and the three women had a rare evening of
rest and companionship. Helen had realised that Geillis
could sing, and play the jaw harp, and they insisted she entertain them, joining in
with gusto as the wine took hold. It was still dark and there was a nip to the air
as Geillis walked home to the Setons' the next morning. She crept through the
cold kitchen and into her room, jumping in fright at the sight of the master and
his son, waiting there in the dark. She tried to run but young David caught her,
and next thing she knew she was locked in the great room.

They came in, after a while, and began to deave her, accusing her of this
evil and that, saying she was a witch and she stayed out of the house every next
night because she went to meet with witches. They said she never was a healer
before and if she was one now, it was because she had made a pact with the
Devil.

Geillis said nothing, no matter how long they kept on at her, for what was
she to say? That she stayed away from the house because the master came to
her room and swived her from when she was fourteen years old? She could
hardly say that, and even less could she tell them she had learned her craft
from Agnes, for she knew that that would be as good as pushing Agnes into the
flames of Hell.

At last, frustrated by her stubborn silence, they took her to another place
she did not know and locked her up there in the dark and cold. Other men came
then, bringing terrible instruments with which they threatened and terrorised
her. Still she would not speak, though they kept her from sleeping for days and
weeks. In the end they took to splintering the fingers of her right hand in their
awful metal contraptions, squeezing and squeezing until she passed out from
the pain. They revived her and began again but she could not speak, only howl
and whimper when they stopped. Next they wrapped a rope around her head
and pulled and twisted until she thought her eyes would burst.

Geillis could not have said how long these depredations lasted; it was
forever and it was no time at all. She thought herself back to Helen's house and
she thought of Dr Cunninghame's belief that the mind can be master of the
body, and she knew she could not betray her friends. But then they stripped

her, in front of all those men, and Seton had his son David shave the hair from her body and reach with his hands into her most private parts to find the mark they said she must have, where the Devil had branded her his own. The master watched with a smile and that broke something in her, and so when they said they knew who her associates were, Agnes Sampson and her daughter Helen and Helen's husband and her children and John Fian of Prestonpans whom they called Dr Cunninghame, she could no longer bear it and she said they were innocent of it all, if they needed her to say that she, Geillis Duncan, was a witch, then she would do it but Agnes was just a healer and Helen not even that, just a wife and mother, and Dr Fian was just schoolmaster with a love of learning who wished to understand the mysteries of life.

After that she had little idea of what she said, for they woke her at strange times of the day and night and shone lanterns in her eyes and accused her of this and that, sailing to the middle of the Forth to raise a storm to kill the king. They spoke no more of her friends but moved on to women she did not know, one called Naper who was the wife of a burgess in Edinburgh and Euphame MacCalzean who was the daughter of Lord Cliftonhall. That one she did know, she said, or she knew of her, she was the goodsister of the master and he hated her, for he believed she had cheated the mistress out of money. They seized on that, questioned her for long hours more, and the next time they came they said she had accused this MacCalzean woman of murder, that she had murdered her father-in-law or her uncle, or perhaps it was both, and a nephew and her husband, although he was alive and so she must have failed, or perhaps it was just that Geillis could not follow, sitting in her filth cradling her broken hand.

They did not stop at Euphame MacCalzean, for by now Geillis understood that King James himself sought to rid himself of inconvenient relations. She was to name the Earl of Bothwell as having attended a Sabbat at North Berwick Kirk – as if Geillis would know the Earl from Adam – where she was to say he kissed the Devil's buttocks. They moved her to the Tolbooth prison then, where she discovered there were six dozen of them, the accused witches, and all arrested on her own say-so.

Among the wretches in the prison were few Geillis knew, but one among them came straight to her and took her in her arms, careful of Geillis's wounds and of her own.

Agnes had been arrested and examined before the king himself at Holyrood. She had been treated as Geillis herself, thrawn with the rope about the head and stripped and searched.

'I didna break,' she told Geillis, 'until they said my son-in-law must suffer too. And then I told them any nonsense they wished to hear.' She barked a laugh. 'Then the king said he didna believe me, for although he has a head full of nonsense himself, it must have seemed a bit much coming from the likes of me. I was near daft with fear then, for if they took Helen's husband then all my bairns would be without protection. And so I said to the king that I could give him evidence if he wished; I could tell him of the private conversation that had passed between him and the queen on their wedding night. And so I did, and he believed me. And they say since I have confessed, they will strangle me before I am burned. And that will be a quick end, which is all any of us can hope for.'

'But how did you know?' Geillis asked. 'What passed between them on their wedding night?'

Agnes laughs until she wheezes. 'What do you think passed between them, lass? She said she knew what they must do but she was afraid, that his member was larger than she expected. The same as has passed between every lad and lass ever wedded who had not the sense or chance to roll in the hay a time or two beforehand to make sure they were well suited.' She laughs again and then must pause for a time to recover from a hacking cough.

Geillis cannot laugh. 'It is my fault you're here,' she says. 'My fault.'

'Wheesht, lass,' says Agnes. 'It's Seton's fault, no other's. Why must women bear the sins of men? Bad enough we bear the children. Wheesht, now, lass, and coorie in. We're together again for now, and I'll do what I can to mend your hands. I've done so before, have I no? Helen brings what she can.'

And Geillis is rocked to sleep in Agnes's arms.

LIVE YOUR LIFE BY GEILLIS

✴ Why do you think the artist who drew Geillis's meeting with King James portrayed Geillis as an older woman?

✴ In your experience, do older women suffer more discrimination in society today?

✴ What do you think of Diana Gabaldon's choice to name a character who practises witchcraft after Geillis?

A NOTE ON GEILLIS'S NAME

Thanks to *Outlander* Geillis is understood to be pronounced with a hard 'g' (as in 'glove'). Given that the name probably derives from the same root as Giles (from Αἰγίδιον or 'young goat'), it may in fact have been pronounced with a soft 'g' (think 'Gillian'). Robert II had a daughter named Egidia who was also known as Gelis; Egidia is from the same root. The Gaelic name Sìleas is sometime associated with Geillis, again suggesting a soft 'g' for Geillis.

"While she never started as a witch, she is a witch now in truth, for has not a woman who has sent her fellow women to the flame truly sold her soul to the Devil?"

BEHIND THE
EYES

FOR MARGARET AITKEN

WHAT WE KNOW

When Margaret Aitken was accused of witchcraft in 1591, she chose to avoid the flames by turning accuser. She convinced her interrogators that she could identify witches by a mark in their eyes, and said she was willing to use this talent in their service, so that they might put more of them to death. The authorities agreed, and Margaret was taken on tour to examine potential witches across the country. She was eventually exposed as a fraud when two women she had condemned were brought before her in different clothing and, failing to recognise them, she made a different judgement. She was taken back to Fife where she was executed.

Margaret's accusations may have increased the numbers executed in the first great 'panic', but her exposure also helped bring that particular outbreak to an end. Her confession was circulated and must have cast doubt among even the most zealous that the basis for convictions was safe.

HOW IT MIGHT HAVE BEEN . . .

THE FLEA BITES FORM a perfect red ring on Margaret's belly, and judging by the burn on her behind, there is another circle of welts rising there too. It is little wonder that the place should be flea-ridden; the straw on the bed is filthy, crushed by the weight of who knows how many strangers, tainted by their sweat, stinking of their excretions, and teeming with the parasites they carry in their filthy travelling clothes. All of the inns in which they have kept her have been slovenly places, but this is by far the worst. The landlord's hands made her shudder, the nails crusted black and the skin ingrained with dirt. The smell of unwashed clothes almost knocked her off her feet, immune as she should be by now.

In childhood, Margaret's mother taught her to mix marigold, lavender and yarrow in with the rushes strewn on the floor, and her bedstraw has never gone more than a season before being changed. At the thought of her mother, Margaret's eyes smart. Long dead though she is, Margaret thinks of her daily. Now, though, she is almost glad Mother is not alive to see how low her daughter has fallen.

Mother was an honest woman, a midwife and a healer, clean and trig and kind. She had a cool, crisp smell about her from the herbs in which she steeped her linen and the tinctures and infusions she used in her work. In these days, perhaps they would have called her a witch too. Did she not aid the occasional woman who sought to slip a bairn, or help end a life once the pain had become unbearable? Once she even drew a living babe from the womb of its dead mother, her heart barely stilled before Mother made her decisive cut.

It was unfortunate that that gory childbed was the first that Margaret had assisted at, aged just twelve, and she immediately determined that it would be the last. She knew that Mother was disappointed; although she never said a word, she would often cast a rueful look at Margaret as she rushed to dress herself in the night whenever there came a knock at the door. Margaret never could meet her eye. In the end Mother took another apprentice, a girl called Jonet. Margaret was surprised by the hot rush of jealousy she felt any time she came across Mother and Jonet, heads bent together over the herbs they were pounding, or a drawing Mother had made in charcoal to show the presentation of a footling babe.

Jonet died of the sweating sickness, one May afternoon in the last year before it disappeared for good. Her father said she had risen in an odd humour that morning, feeling unco and dowie for no reason she could name. She was taken then by a violent fit of the shivers and cried out about an awful pain in her head and her neck. She passed the forenoon in that way, alternately in the grip of the shivers and of the pains. At mid-lowsing time she seemed to rally, released at last from the awful cycle of pain and cold, and said she thought she could take some broth. Once she had drunk it up she said she was hot and a sweat broke out on her brow. It passed soon enough, though, and Jonet said she felt much better, only she was tired and would stretch out on her bed. Only then did her father think to send for Margaret's mother, and he never thought to keep Jonet awake. By the time Mother arrived, she was gone.

Margaret offered to help Mother lay Jonet out, but Mother gave her a sharp look and said she could manage very well by herself, thank you. Margaret drew back, stung, and crept away.

When they came to take Margaret up, more than forty years later, saying she was a witch and an enchantress, a lover of the Devil, she thought on Jonet. Had she desired the other girl's death? Certainly she had wished her gone, out of Mother's affections. Mother mentioned her at the last, Jonet, said she had always felt she had failed her; if only she had been sent for sooner, she would have walked her round and round the room until the sickness had broken.

That was twenty years after Jonet died and even then, a dark stain of envy bloomed through Margaret's breast hearing her name. Had Mother truly loved Jonet so well that she would have risked her own life in that awful sickroom? Margaret was a grown woman by then, of course, and she was immediately ashamed of herself, thinking ill of a girl who died before she was even fully grown. Perhaps her mind was wandering; she had barely slept in those last weeks of Mother's life, sitting up by the bed to tend to her every need. She thought of it as a making of amends.

It was a canker in the breast that killed Mother. As soon as she found the knot under her arm, she said she knew. It took its sweet time, though; or perhaps she fought it, though she said she would not. Margaret was well trained in healing by then, having finally taken her place by Mother's side the year after Jonet died. At the end, when Mother raved and cried aloud in pain, Margaret brewed a strong infusion of nightshade, sweetened with honey, and held it to her lips. Mother's eyes cleared, then, for a second, and looked into Margaret's. She knew. She drank, and lay back in Margaret's arms to await the end.

Margaret thinks often of that last look that passed between them. She has cause to, after all, for is not her trade now looking in the eyes of other women? As once she could have put her hand inside a labouring mother and said how long there was to go, now she can peer into another woman's eye and gauge from the contraction of the pupil whether or not she has secrets to hide. Margaret is quite the expert in twitches and quivers. She sees fear and calls it evil.

This is the bargain she has struck, as once she traded her life for Jonet's to find her way back into Mother's affections. When they accused her, and chained her, they kept her waking for days until she raved and dreamed they were in the cell with her, Mother with her swollen breast and Jonet in her white sweating and that woman they cut open so long ago, struggling to hold her belly together with her hands while all the waters of her womb spilled forth between her fingers and her babe fell blue to the ground. Margaret would have done anything then to escape those spirits and their torment, and so of course she told the elders she was a witch, and moreover she was the very witch of witches, she could look in the eyes of any woman and discern the evil secrets of her soul. They were delighted, the blackguards, and excited even, to have a woman in league with them, accusing her fellow witches while they sat back and ordered the faggots and the rope.

By the time she acquires her flea-ring branding – enough, probably, to condemn another wife as a witch – Margaret has travelled half of Scotland and accused dozens of women. She has peered into an aurora of irises and seen no more than rebellion or anger, fear or worry, pain or sickness; nonetheless she has girded herself and called those women evil. She is weary and sickened, and ashamed, and after a while she glances into those eyes as briefly as she decently can before she looks away and makes her judgement. And so, when they take two women away – women she has condemned as witches – and dress them in new clothes and bring them back, she says they are not guilty, no evil in them, none at all. You would think that one who stared so closely in another's eyes would recognise those same eyes when they peered into them not two hours later. Margaret does not. She has begun to see Mother's eyes instead, or Jonet's, and flinch from their gaze. She no longer knows the difference between a twitch of guilt and the narrowed hardening of disgust.

When they say they will burn her, Margaret is almost relieved, for while she never started as a witch, she is a witch now in truth, for has not a woman who has sent her fellow women to the flame truly sold her soul to the Devil?

Margaret will confess again; this time she will admit she is a fraud. Anything to buy herself the small mercy of strangulation before the horror of the fire.

LIVE YOUR LIFE BY MARGARET

✴ What do you think of what Margaret did?

✴ Do you think anyone can know how they would behave in an extreme circumstance such as Margaret faced? Some people state with confidence that they know they would have taken part in resistance in occupied territories in World War II, for example. Do you think they can know?

✴ What do you think of the willingness of Margaret's accusers to accept her claims?

"There must have been something else I could have done to keep the wolf from the door, is that what you think?"

JUDGE NOT

FOR CHRISTIAN CADDELL

WHAT WE KNOW

While witch trials took place all over Scotland, more activity took place in the Central Belt than elsewhere. The Survey of Scottish Witchcraft database records 32% of accused named witches as being from the Lothians, 14% from Strathclyde and the west, and 12% from Fife. Next in order of number are Borders, Grampian, Tayside, and Highlands and Islands, Caithness, the Northern Isles and Central. In the modern era we think of Central Belt dominance as an issue exacerbated by relative population density, but the early modern population was more evenly distributed across the country and so the numbers are striking.

The county with the highest number of accusations was modern-day East Lothian, then Haddingtonshire. As well as being home to such enthusiastic witch accusers as David Seton Junior and Senior, it was home to one John Kincaid, one of ten or so witch prickers we know were active in Scotland over the period. A description of Kincaid's services survives, from June 1661 in Dalkeith:

" . . . the magistrate and minister caused John Kincaid in Tranent, the common-pricker to prick [Janet Peaston], and found two marks upon her which he called the Devill his marks, which apeared indeed to be so, for she did nather find the prein when it was put into any of the said marks nor did they blood when they were taken out again. And quhan she was asked 'Quhair shoe thoght the preins were put in?' Shoe pointed at a part of her body distant from the place quhair the preins were put in they being preins of thrie inches or thairabout in length. Quhilk Johne Kinkaid declaris upon his oath and verifies by his subscription to be true."

Witch pricking was sometimes done in public and one of these exhibitions may have been the spark that inspired Christian Caddell (or Caldwell) of Newburgh in Fife to take it up as a career. She was barred from doing so as a woman, and so she became 'John Dickson, burgess of Forfar', and was engaged under this name by the Bailie of Spynie to work as a witch pricker in Elgin and environs. As Dickson, Caddell may have been involved in the interrogation of Isobel Gowdie.

Later Caddell would work as 'Paterson the Pricker', under which name she tortured a number of women and men in Strathglass. These unfortunates were caught up in a clan feud and appealed to MacLean of Duart for support. MacLean protested their trials and eventually they were released.

Christian's luck had run out. She was arrested and taken to the Tolbooth Prison in Edinburgh, where she maintained that the pricking had been a sham and instead she had the same skill as Margaret Aitken – to tell a witch by looking in their eyes. She was tried and sentenced to transportation as an indentured servant to the plantations of Barbados and her bond was bought over by a Leith-dwelling Quaker. Thereafter she disappears from the history books.

Christian was not the only cross-dresser in the early-modern Scottish records. A number of records of similar cases exist, and in the main female-to-male cross-dressing seems to have been carried out for practical purposes. In the words of Laura Hedrick of St Andrew's University, 'Female soldiers, pirates and swindlers could exist only when under male guise.'* This was treated as

* 'Male and Female He created them: Counterfeit Masculinity and Gender Presentation as Social Structure in Scotland and England, c.1560 – 1707', Laura E. Hedrick in *Journal of Scottish and Irish Studies* Volume 6 Issue 2 (Aberdeen University Press, 2013)

a crime since such cross-dressing was a means to assume a counterfeit identity. In Christian's case the motive must have been in significant part financial. Witch prickers were among the few people actually to profit from the trials. In Elgin, Christian received 6 shillings a day for her expenses, and 6 pounds Scots for every witch she identified. The maintenance alone was around six times an average wage.

We do not know exactly how many accused witches lost their lives after being pricked by Christian, but the number is likely in the region of six to ten. It might have been significantly higher had MacLean of Duart not intervened in the Strathglass cases. On the day Christian left Scotland for Barbados, Isobel Elder and Isobel Simpson were executed in Forres. Were they her last victims?

READ ON FOR HOW IT MIGHT HAVE BEEN . . .

SEE WHAT YOU THINK OF ME.

Greedy. Conniving. Unnatural. What other words are there for a woman who binds her breast, haps herself in breeches and goes out into the world to hunt for witches?

You may think of me so, if you choose. It does not trouble me.

Perhaps you think I should have starved instead, like those poor souls that have nothing but the scant pickings they may glean from hedgerow or midden. I have seen them often, huddled in their rags behind a dyke or byre, their stick-limbs shaking with ague and their eyes glazed over. They rail, sometimes, against their fate; the mind wanders as the belly gripes on nothing.

I see *you* have always had plenty to eat. All your own teeth, too. Mercy, it was a fine table your folk kept.

There must have been something else I could have done to keep the wolf from the door, is that what you think?

And tell me, what might that have been?

Matrimony is one road for a lass like me, and I set out on it as hopeful as any other, married to a saddler with two trig rooms above his shop. But all that got me was days of drudgery and a nightly beating that cost me four teeth in three years. We had no children – I saw to that – and it was a blessing when the drunken sot took an earache and died. He'd gambled away all we ever had, and he left me with no wish ever to take another man.

Perhaps I could have found a place on a farm or in a fine house, but there were plenty others looking and I had little skill to recommend me. I have no talent for spinning or weaving, I cannot brew. The cow does not let down her milk for me, and my bread is more often scorched than not.

Yes, easy pickings are few and far between for a woman like me. And witch pricking is easy. I know how it's done – who in this kingdom does not? They say a witch has a numb spot somewhere about her person where the Devil has marked her with the sign of their covenant. No matter how this spot is jabbed or pricked, it bleeds not and she feels no pain. The witch pricker shaves her head and her body hair and jabs away with an awl or bodkin until he finds the place,

proving her guilt sufficiently that there is nothing for it but to confess. Kincaid the pricker came to Fife when I was a child and saw to it that many women there died. He lived a fine life for a carle from a family of rapists and poisoners.

Once I had set my mind on it, the hardest part was getting the money together to get my start. Needles and awls I already had – I'd sold most of my husband's kit when he died but held onto a thing or two I thought might come in handy if ever I was reduced to sleeping out of doors. I needed a suit of men's clothes, a hat, a change of linen – naw, two changes, for I could see it wouldn't be the cleanest of work. Once all that was procured, I needed enough silver to get myself somewhere I wasn't known. A tumble or two with a blacksmith of my acquaintance – an elderly widower much missing his wife – and I had what I needed.

I left Fife as Christian Caddell; I rode into the north country as John Dickson. I hadn't chosen the place when I set out; instead I struck north and followed the scent of smoke. Travellers gossip; more than one heading south spoke of witches in the places between Aberdeen and Inverness. I chose Elgin when they told me it was a place of fiery covenanting belief with a cathedral stripped of the lead in its roof and all its carvings and rood screens. Men who so hate the fine works of old often hate women too, I find.

I made my way to the best inn in the place and gave my occupation as witch pricker, my home place as Forfar. It was not two days before a man came calling to summon me to meet with one Innes, Bailie of Spynie. That evening I asked the woman who brought the food about the man. She was a fount of information, as are many folk in these parts. The Inneses were descended from a man named John of Coldreasons, she told me. He was born a bastard, but he had the favour of a great man descended from the first King James himself. With his help Innes was legitimated and the family rose from there. Now they were Bailies of Spynie and heard law cases in the cathedral.

He was most certainly my man.

I did not meet Innes himself in the cathedral the next day, though, but rather a senior man among his clerks. I was hard pressed not to gape when this cove named the fee. Four shillings a day maintenance, he said, and four pounds Scots for every witch I found with my needle. I closed my eyes so he would not see the glint in them, and got up as if to leave.

"With rates like those," I said, "I wonder if thou and thy master are not in league with the witches."

He reddened and I knew I had him, he would not wish to report to his master that the only witch pricker within fifty miles had turned them down. "Six shillings, then," he said. "And six pound Scots for each witch."

I nodded. "Very well."

He doled out the first month's allowance from a strongbox there and then. I dined on a roast chicken that night, and rich, red Spanish wine. It was the first I'd ever tasted, and it made me feel strange, as though I was floating outside my body, watching myself eat and drink. I fell into bed and slept the sleep of the dead.

The contract lasted a year and they put me to work almost right away. A poor woman, the first one, accused of maleficium by those living closest to her. Clear enough to anyone with sense that the charges were invented by a neighbouring wife with a grudge, but in these days there is no sense, and so they tied her to a rope and kept her waking for days and sent for me with my awls and blades.

Better I should do it than a man, no?

I never sought to add to their pain. They were crazed with tiredness, mostly, by the time I was called, and I made sure it was over fast. Jab, jab, jab – not too deep, I'm not a monster, just enough till the blood ran and it looked like the thing – and then I'd find it as fast as I decently could. The witch's mark. A place where she felt nothing, bled not. No surprise that, given that I'd rigged my awl to have one side that collapsed in on itself so it barely touched her.

It's a performance, you understand? The witch is stripped, her body hair shaven. They confess to stop the shame of it. The blade is the end of it, not the beginning.

I was there more than half a year. It's fine country and I saw much of it as I travelled here and there, following the accusations with my kit in a bag on my shoulder. I travelled alone at first, without a man to wait on me, since any waiting man would have quickly discovered my secret. It was lonely at times, I'll admit, but I had no intention of losing my wages to a blackmailer.

You will say that terror followed wherever I went, no doubt. But don't be a fool – not all of those women were innocent. One told me herself she had killed the babes of her master. I knew Kincaid the pricker liked to have an accused murderer touch the corpse of the victim to see if it bled. I had worked out a way of making that seem to happen but sadly many years had passed since those little corpses had gone into the ground and so I never had the chance to try it. A shame.

Things first went wrong for me in Tain, a fine burgh in the shire of Ross. It was a man I was called to prick there, which pleased me some after so many women, but I should have known better. I had passed as Dickson with little trouble all those months, for who would choose to look a witch pricker in the eyes? This one did. Hay, he was called, and he was a messenger to the court. I know not how he came to be accused, but he was not afraid. He looked me full in the eyes and spoke of the law. They nodded to me to proceed, but when I stepped forward Hay grabbed the awl from my hand and tested it. "The blade slides," he cried, showing them. "This carle is a fraud!"

I blustered and threatened and said that the awl was broken. They let me finish with another, but as soon as I was done and able to leave I saddled my horse and rode from the place without so much as collecting my belongings from my lodgings. I always carry my money on my person and shirts are easy to come by – a new neck, less so, when one's own is stretched by the hangman.

I went to Inverness then, where I was able to procure fair lodgings and new linens, and even chanced the hiring of two servants to wait on me. After the disaster in Tain the Sheriff there was seeking my arrest, and so I thought it wise to leave John Dickson behind. I called myself James Paterson, in honour of my mother, who was of that surname. It was in my mind to live quietly there for a time, but I could not rest easy watching my money reduce, and I know of little honest work suitable for a woman dressed as a man. And so I had my man lug in to the tittle-tattle of the taverns, and we came to hear of strife in a place to the south and west called Strathglass. I struck out the next day with my woman servant Isobel.

This was not the same as the other cases I'd pricked. The folk were different, for one, speaking the Erse tongue among themselves. I have not a word of it. They were clannish, too, and not like the cottars in whichever wee village in Fife who think themselves very superior to their neighbours along the road. These ones really did answer to different chieftains. The gang to be accused of witchcraft were MacLeans on Chisolm land,

and it seems the Chisolm chieftain had been looking for them to be gone for some years. The success of the witch finders in the north inspired him, and the ministers and elders of the place were soon busy taking these MacLeans to a place called Wardlaw to be questioned. That's where I came in.

I won't lie, I don't have the stomach for the worst of the witch torture. I stick a few pins in a person, little more than a jealous sister pinching a little brother. These folk suffered in true fashion. They dragged them to prison bound to horses, hung them up by the thumbs, burned the soles of their feet and more. By the time I came to prick them they were poor wretches indeed.

I stripped them in public, in the kirkyard, shaved their heads and pricked them. I made much of looking them over and only stuck the blade in twice to each, in places I knew to cause little pain. I left it in one of them and challenged them to find it. One of the women looked at me with piteous eyes and asked me if I had no heart, to expose her in such a way, in front of the whole community. What man, she asked, would be so cruel as to do so?

By then I think I had almost forgotten I was a woman myself. As Dickson or Paterson I could move freely, go where I wanted, do as I pleased. Being a woman had only ever brought me constriction and pain. My father's hands where they should never have been, *making sure I was becoming a full-grown wife*, as he would have it. Perhaps that is why I found it so easy to leave Christian Caddell lying by the side of the great road north. Would not you have done likewise, if you were me?

I did not answer that woman. I had a job to do, and I did it.

(DON'T) LIVE YOUR LIFE BY CHRISTIAN

★ We do not and cannot know Christian's motivations. The story suggests a number of motivations she might have professed. What do you think?

★ Some commentators suggest that witch prickers were charlatans using knives with retractable blades, similar to stage props, as Christian does in the story. Others suggest this would not have been necessary since the body naturally has spots that are less sensitive to pain or which bleed less. Do you think they might have been charlatans, or not?

★ From a modern perspective, what do you think a 'Devil's mark' might have been? Might you have one?!

A WHIFF
OF SMOKE

B Y THE TIME THE Witchcraft Act was repealed in 1736, official witch-hunts had already died out. The last 'witch' to be executed in Scotland was Janet Horne of Dornoch in 1727 and she, like other victims of the later years, was prosecuted in a local court. Over time central courts had become less convinced of the safety of the evidence used in the trials, such as confessions obtained under torture, and they became increasingly wary of involvement. Moves towards Enlightenment values of reason saw practices such as witch pricking re-evaluated as fraudulent. In 1736 witchcraft was abolished as a crime and a new Witchcraft Act instead illegalised 'pretended witchcraft'. It would remain on the statute books until 1951, when it was replaced by the Fraudulent Mediums Act. The last person imprisoned under the 1736 Act was a Scottish woman, Helen Duncan, in 1944.

Does the repeal of the Act, though, mean that belief in witchcraft ceased? It certainly did not turn off like a tap.

A decade after the Act was repealed, a woman was tortured to death in Skye on the basis – at least ostensibly – that her killer thought she was practising witchcraft with the intention of doing him harm.

Over a hundred years later, in 1894, Edinburgh luminary Patrick Geddes had a small fountain installed on the Castle Hill in Edinburgh as a memorial to those who died there. Geddes and the designer John Duncan seem to have accepted that the victims were actually witches, stating that, 'some used their exceptional knowledge for evil purposes while others were misunderstood and wished their kind nothing but good.'

In popular culture, writers and dramatists frequently draw on victims of witchcraft persecutions in Scotland and elsewhere in narratives that similarly characterise these people (mainly the women) as actually witches. *Outlander* is one example. The 1993 film *Hocus Pocus* is another, in which a boy named Max moves to Salem with his family and accidentally awakens a trio of witches.

The image of the witch persists more broadly, too, and it is frequently used as a shorthand for 'woman'. In a demonstration against the carbon policy of Australian Prime Minister Julia Gillard in 2011, campaigners held up signs reading

'Ditch the Witch'. When Hilary Clinton stood in the US presidential election in 2016 she was regularly caricatured as a witch. It may be that powerful or outspoken women are particularly characterised in this way as a means to reinforce cultural norms that require women to mind their language, stay in their lane, be kind. Powerful women may be doubly vulnerable to such characterisation because their power is resented, and they are visible. Their treatment acts as a warning to their sisters across society.

Nineteenth-century American writer and activist Matilda Joslyn Gage believed 'witch' had an even broader application. Gage proposed a thought experiment in which the word 'woman' is replaced wherever it occurs with the word 'witch'. Viewed in this way, witchcraft persecutions are primarily an expression of misogyny. The history of witches is the history of women, and women are witches. A brief dip into Twitter on any given day certainly suggests the latter view persists in many parts of society, and it appears that the platforms on which its adherents publish condone its expression even in the most abusive terms.

While the crime of witchcraft has been long confined to history in Scotland and broader Western society, it is important to note that witchcraft persecutions persist in some parts of the world today. Typically these follow the same pattern as the historic Scottish persecutions, in the sense that they target the vulnerable in society, and very often women. The Witches of Scotland campaign argues that this renders it particularly important that we secure official recognition that the persecutions in our own history were an injustice.

In the following pages you will find three women – two real-life individuals and one fictional – from different eras in Scotland's history. They were not prosecuted as witches but it might be said that the smoke from the burnings clung to them nonetheless.

"It may be that powerful or outspoken women are particularly characterised in this way as a means to reinforce cultural norms that require women to mind their language, stay in their lane, be kind."

"'S minig, minig, minig thig Crìosda an riochd a' chòigrich."

Often, often, often, Christ comes in the guise of a stranger.

THE FIRE A MAN MAKES FOR HIMSELF
(AN TEINE A NÌ DUINE DHA FHÈIN)

FOR KATHERINE MACKINNON /
DO CHATRÌONA NICFHIONGHUIN

WHAT WE KNOW

Katherine MacKinnon died in 1747 in Duisdale Beag in Sleat, in Skye, twelve days after being attacked at a house in nearby Camuscross. Court records show that one Ruairidh Mac Iain MacDonald, a tacksman of Clan MacDonald of Armadale, was charged with her 'barbarous and cruel murder'. MacDonald was accused of tying her hands and burning her feet over a fire as he sought to extract a confession for what he alleged was witchcraft, an attempt to poison his men and cause other mischief about his property. Katherine was a beggar who had approached his house to seek help.

The Camuscross attack happened more than ten years after the repeal of the Witchcraft Act under which witch-hunting had been made legal. In common with formal persecutions, however, it happened in a community witnessing significant social change and tension. The first of two main phases of clearances were affecting the Highlands, the clan system was in rapid decline and there were significant implications for the tacksman class to which MacDonald belonged.

Tacksmen leased their 'tack' of land from the clan chief – to whom they were often related – and then sublet it to peasant farmers and their families. These tenants raised cattle the clan would trade, and the profits would be offset against their rent. Tacksmen accordingly had a significant level of power over their subtenants. When the clan system was in full swing, this might have been a benevolent power, but by the time MacDonald was accused of Katherine's murder, the dynamic was changing. Increasingly clan chiefs saw themselves as landlords rather than as patriarchs and protectors of their people ('clann' literally means 'children'). Under this new understanding, their tacksmen became agents enforcing financial exploitation. The ability of Highland farmers to live off the land was often fragile at best. Without the protection of their chief, and indeed under heavy rents from that quarter, many found it impossible.

Ruairidh Mac Iain was accused of Katherine's murder, but he was not convicted.

HERE'S HOW IT MIGHT HAVE HAPPENED . . .

I T HAS BEEN A RAW, hard, hungry day and, although it is still quite early, Mòrag has retreated to her bed as it is the only place she will feel warm right through. She heard a story last week about the great hero Cù Chulainn killing his own son by mistake and her intention is to lie in the dark with her eyes closed and tell it to herself again. But the house is dark, the cat curls up beside her and of course the inevitable happens and she is sound asleep when Allan brings the old woman home. The first she is aware, the limp body is slumped beside her in the bed. She shakes her head, slow to wake and struggling to understand what is happening.

'Bha i na sìneadh air an t-sitig,' Allan's voice says. 'Tha i cho fuar ris a' phuinnsean.' *She was lying in the midden; she's as cold as ice.*

Mòrag puts her hand to the body's cheek and almost snatches it back. The skin is as cold as that of any corpse; Allan has brought a dead woman home. But as they peer through the darkness, there is an awful noise from the body, halfway between a moan and a gasp. The sound breaks the spell that has bound Mòrag and she clambers out of bed.

'Cuir fon phlaide i,' she says. *Put her under the covers.* She helps Allan to cover the old woman, tells him to make up the fire and set water to boil. She lights the oil in the crùisgean and hangs it as close as she can to the bed so she can see. She takes the old woman's hands from under the covers and chafes them between her own, first one and then the other. She has some hurt or other around her wrists, where the skin is broken and bruised. Mòrag is careful to avoid those places as she rubs, up and down from the hands to the elbows and then to and fro across the upper arms.

Soon the fire is glowing and the room begins to acquire a smoky warmth. When the water has boiled, Mòrag pours a bowl and waits until it is cool enough to bear. Then she dips a cloth in it and holds it to the old woman's skin, pressing in the warmth, dipping it back in the bowl as it cools, pouring in another ladle of hotter water again whenever the bowl itself begins to lose its heat. As she works, Allan slips outside, saying he has something he must fetch.

Mòrag's intention is to only warm the woman, but as she works, she sees that her efforts are also cleaning away the glaur that cakes her. The poor rags that clothe her are sodden and filthy, and Mòrag strips them off as she goes. There is nothing she can do about the matted hair. She takes a clean shift of her own from the kist and lifts the old woman to dress her in it. She is as light as a child, as fragile as a bird. They are all thin this year, for the weather has not been kind, but this woman is little more than bone.

''S minig, minig, minig,' Mòrag whispers, 'thig Crìosda an riochd a' chòigrich.' *Often, often, often, Christ comes in the guise of a stranger.*

The old woman is still very pale but the greenish tinge that coloured her jaw is gone now, her lips are less blue. Mòrag can hear her breathing now, fragile stitches of the thread that binds her to life.

'Chan eil grèim bidhe againn a bheir sinn dhuibh,' Mòrag says to her. *We have no food to give you.*

The woman says nothing; Mòrag is not sure she can hear. In the morning – if she sees the morning – Mòrag will brew a stew of nettles to feed her, or of dulse. That will help sustain her without giving her poor stomach too much too soon – she is clearly unaccustomed to meat or milk. At the thought of food, Mòrag's own empty belly gripes.

Just then Allan comes in with a bundle he sets on a stool and opens. There are oatcakes, a large piece of white cheese, a string of dried fish.

'Bho Ealasaid,' Allan says. *From Elizabeth.*

Mòrag's eyes fill with tears of relief. This is bounty indeed; supplemented with dulse and nettles, wild garlic and silverweed, this will keep them going until Allan can harvest the barley, it will keep them fed until the poultice Mòrag has made for the cow's udder has had a chance to work. Mòrag fervently hopes it will work.

Allan's eyes turn to the old woman and Mòrag sees that he is worried Ealasaid's bundle will not be enough to save them if they have an extra mouth to feed. Mòrag thinks the gift may have come for this very reason, God helping them extend hospitality to this poor soul for as long as she may need it.

''S minig, minig, minig,' she says, for the second time tonight, 'thig Crìosda an riochd a' chòigrich.'

Allan nods. He peers at the old woman.

'Chunna mi roimhe i,' he says. *I've seen her before.* 'Air an deirc.' *Begging.*

'Bha i shìos mu Chamus Croise an-dè.' *She was down by Camuscross yesterday.*

Mòrag is not surprised; life here is precarious and the woman would not be the first poor widow reduced to walking from township to township, begging for the charity of her neighbours. She tucks the blankets tenderly around the thin shoulders and moves to lift them from the woman's feet so she can begin her washing at the other end. Allan helps by holding up a glowing end of peat. What Mòrag sees by the light, she cannot understand.

The woman's feet are burned bloody and black, more like meat than feet. The toes are not all there, or perhaps they have been melded together by the fire that has burned them. She cannot possibly have stood on them; she must have been thrown or crawled onto their sitig. Mòrag pulls Allan down to see and he gags.

After a brief conference, they decide to lay wet strips of linen on the feet. Honey might help, Mòrag thinks, but they have none. Once they have laid the wet cloths on, they place the blankets gently down but the old woman groans and they lift them again. They are torn then by the need to keep her warm and to spare her the pain that the weight of the blankets brings. In the end Alan places a pot on one side of her and a stool on the other and they tent the blankets over her like that.

The old woman seems to be asleep now, warm enough and not apparently dying for the moment, and so Mòrag and Allan make a bed for themselves on the floor by the fire with blankets and cloaks and a sack of fleece waiting to be spun. They whisper in low voices of the woman's dreadful injuries. She must have walked into a fire, Allan says, in drink or crazed with hunger and exhaustion. But Mòrag thinks of the marks on her wrists and says she thinks her hands may have been tied together, like a fetter on the legs of a cow. Neither knows what to make of that and they fall into silence. Mòrag whispers a prayer of healing and falls into an uneasy sleep.

When they rise at dawn, the woman is alive, and warm, but it is the warmth of fever and her skin is damp and sweaty. Mòrag sends Allan to see if he can find elderflower and mint to brew, to bring the fever down. While he is gone, she redresses the feet, gingerly lifting the wet linen from the awful burns, wetting it once more and laying it back on. It seems kinder to do this while the woman is asleep; Mòrag will have to rouse her soon so she can drink. Even without fever, a body will surely die without water.

When Allan returns with such leaves and flowers as he has found, they brew the drink and attempt to rouse the woman, raise her up and spoon it into her mouth. Her eyes never focus but she takes in a little and they lay her down again. She drifts back into sleep, or perhaps she is unconscious.

Allan is out with the rest of the township at the peats all day and so Mòrag passes the long hours alone with the woman, going about her own work, stopping every now and then to spoon more liquid into her patient's mouth and moisten the dressings on her feet. The woman barely rouses, but Mòrag thinks her skin is cooler to the touch. In the late afternoon, though, she becomes agitated, crying and sobbing and repeating broken sentences over and over again. In the end Mòrag climbs into bed with her, careful not to jostle her poor feet, and moulds herself to her side. The woman quietens and slips back into sleep.

When Allan comes home in the evening, he has a dark look on his face. Mòrag knows better than to ask him straight out what is troubling him; she has learned through long experience that he will come to it in his own time. She has stewed nettles and garlic to eat with one of Elizabeth's oatcakes and a slice of the cheese, and as they chew Allan tells her that there was much talk at the peats, disturbing chatter about Ruairidh Mac Iain, MacDonald of Armadale's tacksman at Camuscross. He is known to be a difficult man, quick to take offence or raise a quarrel. More than once has a man in Sleat left his company bruised, bloody, or slashed with a blade.

Folk are saying that the tacksman, deep in drink, accused a beggarwoman of witchcraft. He found her outside his house and accused her of plotting against him and his men, planning to poison them. They say he hauled her into the house, bound her and held her feet to the fire, demanding that she confess. She howled and screamed as they burned her, but denied any ill will against MacDonald, maintaining she only ever meant to ask for his help. MacDonald continued to torment her for a time until he became bored. His men, by then, had perhaps become uneasy; someone untied the woman and dumped her by the road to Isle Oronsay. From there she must have crawled to Duisdale Beag, where Allan found her. A couple of MacDonald's men have ridden off, they say, ashamed perhaps of what they were party to, or afraid of the consequences.

'Dè an t-ainm a th' oirre, an tuirt iad?' asks Mòrag. *What's her name, did they say?*

Her name is Catrìona NicFhionghuin – Katherine MacKinnon. It somehow seems easier to care for her now they know it. They call her by her name and her eyes open. They feed her some of the nettle stew, and although she can eat little, she tries, and she swallows more of the infused water than she has before. They speak to her now as they change the dressings on her feet and, while her pain is great, she turns her face to the wall and bears it.

Mòrag is haunted by the story they have heard of Katherine's torment. She is afraid of the tacksman of Camuscross, who is a man of some power. Will he find out that Katherine is here? She is afraid he might come to end the job he has started. What price will she and Allan pay for sheltering the evidence of the tacksman's crime?

Allan says he has said nothing to anyone about Katherine, but the neighbours know, for while no one comes into the house, Mòrag finds a steady stream of gifts on the doorstep. Fish, milk, herbs, honey, butter, even a large piece of meat. Mòrag's eyes are wet when she finds these offerings, for no one here has much at all to spare. The evil of their tacksman fades a little against the kindness of the township.

A week after she arrived, Katherine seems to rally a little, talking to them in a cracked voice and eating an oatcake and some cheese. But Mòrag is worried about her feet. She has applied the neighbours' honey to the burns morning and night, but the toes have blackened. As the second week progresses, Katherine sleeps more and more and dark red streaks appear on her legs, leading upwards from her ankles. In desperation, Allan brings Ealasaid, who has some knowledge of healing. Ealasaid looks at the feet with pursed lips. She speaks a low word of prayer to Katherine and goes out for a long time. When she returns she has a bag of leaves Mòrag does not know.

'Tha puinnsean san fhuil,' she says to Mòrag in a whisper. 'Cha dèanar sion dhi tuilleadh.' *The poison is in her blood.* There is nothing you can do. She tells Mòrag how it will progress; she has seen such a death before. She says the leaves will help hasten the end, brewed strong in water. Sweeten it with honey, she counsels, and she will go peacefully to her eternal rest.

On the twelfth day Mòrag knows the time has come. Katherine's pain is great and Mòrag brews the leaves and cools the drink. Once Katherine has drunk it, Mòrag sits with her and holds her hand, wetting her lips now and then with water and honey. Gradually the rictus of agony leaves her face. Her heartbeat slows, and her breath rattles in her chest. She rears up a moment in panic, but Mòrag soothes her and helps her down. Katherine closes her eyes and she is gone.

That night Allan and Mòrag make their decision. They will report the tacksman for his crime and then they will wait. If they must, then they will pack their gear and make their way from this place where they have lived, and their ancestors have lived, since time immemorial. They trust that as they encircled Katherine and cared for her, the Lord will guard them should their pursuit of justice cast them into a howling waste of wilderness.

LIVE YOUR LIFE BY KATHERINE

✳ Do you think there was a gendered element to the violence against Katherine?

✳ Katherine's abuser was not convicted despite the apparent existence of witnesses. Do you see any parallels with the prosecution of violence today?

✳ Do you see any parallels between Katherine's experiences and homelessness today? (In December 2021 0.57% of households in Scotland did not have a home of their own.)

"chan eil e muigh,
's chan eil e staigh,
's cha tig an taigh
às aonais."

Neither outside, nor inside,
but every house that is a
house must have one.

THE WOMAN IN THE STONES

DO MHÀIRI NIGHEAN ALASDAIR RUAIDH /
FOR MARY MACLEOD

WHAT WE KNOW

Màiri nighean Alasdair Ruaidh (Mary MacLeod) was born in Rodel, in Harris in the late 1500s. She was never accused or convicted of witchcraft, as far as we know. But oral tradition says she was buried face-down, under stones, in an echo of a Norse custom for the disposal of the remains of a witch. Tradition also says that the same treatment was given to the remains of another woman born a hundred years later in a different part of Gaelic Scotland, Mairead (sometimes Mairearad) nighean Lachlainn.

Màiri and Mairead might, of course, have received perfectly standard burials of the time. So why does oral tradition remember them in this strange way?

Both women were poets. Màiri is the better known, reckoned as a major poet of her age. Her father 'Red Alasdair' was said to be descended from the MacLeod chiefs of Harris and Skye, and Màiri served as nursemaid to the family of her kinsman MacLeod of MacLeod at Dunvegan Castle. In Gaelic society poetry played a specific function in promoting the political interests of the clan and most of the songs Màiri composed (Gaelic poetry was an oral tradition) were of this type, although she also composed work in the women's song tradition.

Oral tradition has it that Màiri and her poetry were suppressed. She is said to have composed on the threshold since she belonged neither to the tradition of women – whose songs were made for private spaces and gatherings – nor to the great public tradition normally practised by men. She is also supposed to have dismissed one of her own poems when objection was taken by saying *'chan eil ann ach crònan.'* 'It's only a lullaby.'

More seriously still, Màiri was exiled at some point to the small island of Scarba, across the Corryvreckan whirlpool from the Isle of Jura. We know this because she tells us so in one of her songs. We think there had been a fracture in her relationship with Roderick MacLeod of MacLeod (d. 1654), perhaps because Màiri was too quick to praise Roderick's cousin Norman MacLeod of Berneray in her songs. Relations were mended when Iain Breac ('Speckled John') succeeded his brother and Màiri was once again installed at Dunvegan.

Màiri is said to have returned home to Rodel to live out her last years, and to have been buried there at St Clement's Church, which was built for the MacLeods in the years before the Reformation and fell into disuse shortly thereafter. St Clement's has within its eastern wall a strange exhibitionist carving of a woman broadly considered to be of a type known as a 'Sheela-na-gig'. We don't entirely understand the history of these odd carvings, and we don't know whether they were better understood in Màiri's time. The woman at Rodel has weathered to a degree that makes her particularly mysterious.

READ ON FOR HOW IT MIGHT HAVE BEEN . . .

I WAS FOND OF RIDDLES and conundrums as a child and my father delighted in sharing the many he knew. The first I ever solved for myself was the riddle of the door – 'chan eil e muigh, 's chan eil e staigh, 's cha tig an taigh às aonais.' *Neither outside, nor inside, but every house that is a house must have one.* Once I had solved it, of course, I posed it to anyone who would listen, and I have taught it to dozens of children in my care.

Perhaps it is apt that I love that riddle so well, since many of my countryfolk have come to say that the doorway was my place, the spot where I could stand and make my poems. I am supposed to have claimed so myself, to outwit a judgement of my chief. He is said to have decreed that a woman – a nursemaid no less! – had no business making songs in praise of chief and clan but instead should compose ditties for the nursery or laments for lost love. In this way I might pass my time while I darned his children's stockings, or help keep the rhythm as the women pounded the waulking board. It is the role of men to compose poetry for the great world outside, you see, to inspire valour in battle or melt the resolve of an enemy in the heat of the poet's scorn. In this version of events I am a creature in between, a woman making men's poetry and so – the story goes – I took up position on that threshold, the better to make songs that had no place inside among the women or out among the men. My chief is supposed to have responded by exiling me for my pains.

I claimed no such thing, in truth, and he passed no such judgement, but I do not mind the stories, for in many ways am I not a creature of the spaces in between? Born in one island but passing my life in another, my heart forever reaching north and west across that great expanse of sea. A MacLeod through my father's people and a MacDonald through my mother's, I served the greatest branch of my father's clan while the ties of kinship and plain good sense bound me more closely to another. And does a nursemaid herself not stand on a threshold of sorts? She ushers children into adulthood, of course, but often, too, she stands in the shadow Death would cast over childbed and cradle. I have nursed five lairds of MacLeod and two of Applecross and lost not one of them, but I have wrapped other small souls in linen, bound not for fosterage in some great house, but for a colder lodging in the grave.

Sir Roderick's children survived the nursery and my care, but still his son did not outlive him. Perhaps this helped make up his mind to send me into exile, for what man can entirely hold his reason when his children go to their graves before him? He was sad, and I was fiery, and took pride in the power of my words and my wit. I confess I did not always spare him the sharp side of my tongue. I was his kinswoman after all, and I thought to help him see the occasional error of his ways. I saw my means to do so in the example of his great cousin in Berneray, and I made many songs that sought to inspire him to follow in Sir Norman's footsteps. As I might have known, Sir Roderick was not minded to have his kinswoman-bard lecture him in this way, not least since he thought himself the greater MacLeod. Before I knew it, I was on board a galley sailing for Mull, on to Jura and finally to the smallest and roughest prison of all, across the great whirlpool of Corryvreckan to the scrap of an island they call Scarba. My anger churned for a time, but word of his death rent my heart regardless. When his brother Iain Breac succeeded him and recalled me to Dunvegan, I carried with me a fine lament for Roderick, and with it I took my place again in that glorious household. The great MacCrimmon pipers flourished, a fool capered and I made my songs alongside the great blind harper-bard from the Isle of Lewis. I dwelled in favour in that place then, and I ensured my fires were banked so that my words should never flare up and burn me again.

I am old now, and my fires gone out. I am too infirm to be of use in the nursery at Dunvegan or anywhere else, and so I have returned to Harris, to Rodel where I began. I wake in the morning light of heart and when I have leisure and strength I walk, once again coming to know this land of my father's and my father's fathers back to the time of Pharaoh. I have visited the old church many times, and I find it peaceful to walk among so many of my kindred, resting quiet in their graves. The great chieftain Alasdair Crotach lies inside the nave in a strange archway carved with angels, priests of the old times in their odd robes and hats and pictures of hunting and sailing. There is a castle that must be Dunvegan, but having spent my life there I can only conclude the mason had never seen it.

Alasdair is carved in full armour, as is his son William, but their effigies interest me less than the woman carved outside, in the east wall of the tower. I know not quite what to make of her. She holds a small creature and what I think may be a flag. She sits with her thighs apart and there is a *clais* between her legs, a cleft, clear for all to see. Used as I am to attending at childbeds, when first I saw her I thought her a woman newly delivered of a child, but then I wondered why such a thing would be carved into a church even in the times of the old churchmen and their heresies. Peering harder, I am not even sure it is a babe she cradles; it looks more like a dog or perhaps a lamb. I asked a cousin who has always lived here what she was made to tell us, but he says the old beliefs and old ways must be ashes in our memories now, and he can no longer say.

It tickles me, though, to see that woman. I cannot decide whether she is the opposite of me, keeping guard outside in the air and wind while the dead chieftains slumber in the darkness indoors. Or perhaps she is like me instead, in the story where I compose my work in the doorway, neither inside nor out. Set into the walls she, too, occupies a place between. I will lie in the graveyard here when my own time is over and it pleases me that she will watch over me, my eternal sister inside the stones.

LIVE YOUR LIFE BY MÀIRI

★ Why do you think there was resistance to women taking part in the poetry tradition?

★ Do you see any echoes of this in the modern era?

★ More broadly, to what degree do you think we have 'equal rights' today?

"So there we were, having the illicit time of our lives, when that drunken sot O' Shanter keeked in the window . . ."

CUTTY SARK

FOR 'NANNY'

WHAT WE KNOW

The prurient elements of the witchcraft accusations – women fornicating with the Devil, causing erections in their neighbours, etc. – remained in the public consciousness long after the persecutions ended. Arguably they still do. When Robert Burns picked up his pen to create the supernatural shenanigans of *Tam o' Shanter*, he drew from this deep wellspring. Tam is almost bettered by a young witch dancing in a short shift to whom he immediately takes a fancy.

Burns first published *Tam O' Shanter* in the *Edinburgh Herald* and the *Edinburgh Magazine* in 1791. He then gave the poem to Francis Grose for inclusion in his *Antiquities of Scotland*, in which Burns had previously suggested Grose include an etching of Alloway Kirk. Grose had agreed, on condition that Burns provide text to accompany the image. Burns provided *Tam* alongside two other witch tales associated with Alloway Kirk which he called 'authentic'. Tam was rather to eclipse the others, and indeed it went on to become one of the most famous pieces of writing in the world. Tam gave his name to hats, tobacco and Ada Lovelace's horse. Nanny – the comely witch in the short shift – has given her epithet to boats, bars and more.

Burns treated the many women in his real life fairly abominably but some could withstand his charms – one Jean Gardner, for example, chose to pursue a religious life within a sect known as the 'Buchanites' over a relationship with Rabbie. The sect had been established by one Elspeth

Buchan, who claimed many gifts of prophecy and the ability to confer the Holy Ghost on her followers with her breath. In common with many such groups Buchanites were a Doomsday cult and believed that Elspeth would convey them safely to Heaven in the coming apocalypse. Burns gave a scathing account of them. He preferred his superstition strictly fictional.

HERE IS HOW IT MIGHT HAVE BEEN . . .

N*ANNY; I'VE ALWAYS HATED THAT NAME.*
I see myself more as an *Anna*. An *Anna* could be a belle, could marry a lawyer, maybe, or a doctor or an army captain. Perhaps an *Anna* could even be a woman of substance in her own right, a thinker, a writer.

A *Nanny*? Well, at best, a blacksmith's wife. At worst, a goat.

Mother's sister was called Anna. She ran off to join Elspeth Buchan down at Closeburn when I was a child. We don't speak of her at home, Grannie makes sure of that. But I know what they believe, that crowd, everybody does. They believe that Elspeth Buchan is a saint, even though it's clear to anyone with eyes that she's nothing more than a fat fraud from somewhere in the North-East with sweat stains on her bodice and dirty feet. Auntie Anna and her fellow fools once fasted on Buchan's say-so for forty nights and forty days because they believed it would make them light enough to be lifted up to Heaven by the angels. She's a big woman, Auntie Anna. Wouldn't fancy the angel's chances. We're all well-built, the womenfolk in our family, made for living on farms, helping our husbands stook the harvest, or haul a calf out of its mother when things go wrong.

So. No chance my family would ever call me Anna, after Auntie Anna's transgression. It's *Nanny* all the way for me.

Grannie's an *Effie*. Euphemia. The very image of respectability and holiness. When they were pouring out the milk of human kindness, Grannie didn't get her fair share; the woman would as soon take a hairbrush to your legs as give you a smile. I was feared of her when I was young. She never let me forget that I was a sinner. By the time I was thirteen I was a bundle of panic, convinced I was bound for Hell.

My sins were not so many, looking back now, but then I would have said I was a liar (I once denied all knowledge of a broken crock of sugar), a blasphemer (in my head, mainly) and vainer than any Jezebel. On this latter count, you see, I had fallen in love with a dress. It hung in the window of a dressmaker's house in the village, white and yellow striped cotton with a fine green edging, and I coveted it as I had never coveted anything before. It was two pounds Scots – more money than I could ever imagine having in my possession.

I was about to turn fourteen, then, and my monthly bleeding had just begun. Perhaps Grannie was moved by the fact that her last grandchild was so nearly grown, for she said she wished to buy me something special to mark the day of my birth. Something to wear, she said, as soon I might wish to go out among people and I would need something decent to hap myself in.

I was in raptures; it must be the dress.

I didn't sleep the night before my birthday, I was that excited. By the time my parents and Grannie had risen and breakfasted, I was fit to be tied. Finally Grannie handed me the bundle and I almost tore it apart to find—

A Paisley sark.

That's right. My very own full-length woollen woman's undergarment, in Paisley pattern. I don't know about you, but to me nothing says 'wear me against your skin' better than a nice thick woolly shift. And as Grannie said, a woollen sark is always useful: you can wear it under your frock on a cold day, sleep in it, and if the worst happens, you can be laid out in it and wear it for all eternity.

'On the Day of Judgement,' Grannie said, 'you could be proud to stand before your Maker in that sark.' (I've already said she was a fell religious woman; you can make up your own mind about her approach to dressing for big occasions.)

I'll admit I was less than gracious about my gift. Mother wormed her hand under my arm and pinched me, hard.

'Whit bonnie, Mither,' she said to Grannie. 'Is it no bonnie, Nanny?'

'Awfy bonnie,' I said, as enthusiastically as I could.

Grannie looked gratified. 'Twa punnd Scots, yon cost me,' she said. 'T'was a' my riches.'

I could have grat. And maybe I would have, if I'd realised then that that pointed wee comment about the cost would mean that I would be expected to wear the bloody thing for at least another decade.

When I was fifteen I sprouted, so my legs stuck out from the sark like stalks of parsley. Mother let down my two dresses as best she could, but still my ankles jutted out, bony and gangly. Grannie tutted at me and said it wasn't natural for a lass to grow so tall.

That's how I got into the witching. I was desperate to stop growing and my pal Helen said that old wife Morton's niece Mary would give me a charm for it.

I went and asked her one day when Mother had no need of me. Mary laughed at me.

'Wha tauld thou I would hae a thing like thon?' she asked.

'Abody says thou is a witch,' says I. (I was no dissembler at that point in my life.)

'Come to the kirk,' says she then. 'The morn's nicht at full muin.'

I stole out of the house when the rest were asleep and walked to Alloway Kirk. I was a wee bittie nervous, to tell the truth, for it was a cloudy night and there was precious little moonlight to see by. I had no fancy to be jumped on by some bogle or – worse – some randy auld fool like Wullie Fisher. I had no idea either what Mary might bid me do when I reached the kirk.

It turned out she mainly wanted to introduce me to her pals, who said they were a coven of witches and giggled a lot. They sat in a circle and passed round a bottle of rosehip wine and talked about lads that had caught their eye. Then they played a sort of game where they asked a question, cast a ruckle of wee bones down on the ground and then tried to divine what was meant by the pattern in which they fell. You know the sort of thing; I'll wager you've been at least once to a party where someone has asked the spirits for guidance.

The answers they got seemed to me mainly to be the ones they wanted. Towards the end there was a spat as two lasses had an eye on the same lad and each lass maintained the bones were saying she would have him. All was made up in the end, though, and there was some singing before we all wound our way tipsily back home, only to rise bleary-eyed and wabbit not two hours later.

We had arranged the next meeting before we left, at full moon the next month. This time Mary said we'd meet in the kirk itself, and we'd have a dance. She was full of plans to dress the old place up with bones and cobwebs and all sorts. That was Mary all over; you know the type, in love with the idea of darkness and drama.

So there we were, having the illicit time of our lives, when that drunken sot O' Shanter keeked in the window. I suppose it's funny, in a way, but at the time I thought it would put paid to our fun and I was a bit sore. What he said about us after, though, it did tickle me. But let's take the opportunity to set the record straight.

Auld Nick was not in attendance, whatever you've heard. It's dark up there at the winnock bunker, and O' Shanter was drunk. It's funny really that he saw

Jamie Dunlop on the pipes and mistook him for the Devil. Jamie's an unkempt chiel, especially his eyebrows, but 'in shape o beast'? I think that's a bit mean.

Nor was the altar strewn with evidence of murder and mayhem. 'Five scimitars wi murder crusted', indeed. How many houses round the toun of Ayr contain a scimitar, may I ask you? I'll warrant it's many fewer than five. Tomahawks likewise; we have few American natives here. Supposedly there was all sorts else too; a garter which a babe had strangled, a knife a father's throat had mangled. Tell me, how can a man look on a knife and know it has done a murder? He even looked at the ox tongue Christina Smith had brought for her dinner and said it was a lawyer's tongue, turned inside out.

The garter was Betty Dunlop's and she had taken it off in a most scandalous manner. They were all worldly-wise young ladies, Mary's pals, and I felt out of place among them, a parsley-legged stripling of fifteen. I had no knowledge of Jezebel dancing and flirting with men. And so that's when I hit on my plan.

After one dance – it was a reel – I fanned myself ostentatiously and said I thought I might faint.

'Loosen your bodice,' said Mary.

'I'll do better than that,' says me, and I stripped off my whole dress so I stood there in the Paisley sark. It looked quite the racy number then, with my long white legs poking out to the thigh.

There was a great cheering then and everybody else was soon casting off their own skirts and bodices. We got back to the dancing, and it was a wild sight, all those legs and bubbies bouncing and jostling about in time to the tune. The dirty bugger at the window had his hands in his breeches, I'll wager.

It was me in particular that had caught his eye, it seems, for right when we were in the midst of the Strip the Willow – my favourite of all the dances, although the kirk was narrow for it – he cried out something about my cutty sark. The music stopped then and we all ran after him, and the sumph lumbered away and onto his horse. I'm a good runner, with my long legs, and I nearly caught him. The others whooped and howled, but as he reached the old brig, half of his horse's tail came away in my hand. It must have had mange, the poor beast.

When he'd gone we thought we'd better pack up. We had no doubt that would be the end of our fun in Alloway Kirk, once the story got about, but Jamie said he knew a place out by the shore at Carrick where we could meet the next month. I could hardly wait. It's a fine thing to be young.

Oh, the next day I took O' Shanter's wife Kate an ointment for mange; I felt bad about the horse and it's Kate's horse, really. It's a nice beast and Kate's a nice woman. Not her fault her husband's a peeping Tom and a pervert.

LIVE YOUR LIFE BY NANNY

★ Nanny's 'witching' is essentially a teenage rebellion or perhaps a subculture she joins. Teenagers often identify strongly with subcultures. Why do you think this might be?

★ Do you think teenagers today have a different experience from your own?

★ Nanny says that Tam is a peeping Tom. Voyeurism still exists today – and now recording devices facilitate the making of records by the perpetrator. Flashing and other offences also remain common. Why do you think these crimes persist? Are they 'minor' issues?

THE FIRE WITHIN

MOST ANALYSES OF WITCHCRAFT persecutions recognise that there were no actual witches. Instead scholars and writers attempt to untangle the religious, social and political context for the persecutions and/or to explain the emergence of the ideas that underpinned the concept of witchcraft at the time. Additionally the persecutions provide material to social historians and/or those who specifically study women's history, including the history of violence/sexual violence against women.

There are, however, other lenses for viewing witchcraft and some of these attempt to weave the persecutions into a broader narrative of continuity of practice. This approach was first proposed by early twentieth-century feminist, archaeologist and folklorist Margaret Murray, the first woman appointed to lecture in archaeology in Britain. Murray was initially focused on digging in Egypt and writing and speaking on Egyptology at home in England, but the advent of the First World War rather interrupted her work. Instead Murray turned to folklore and anthropology, developing a thesis that there was a tradition of European witchcraft, in which some of the accused genuinely participated. Murray proposed that what they were actually practising was an ancient pagan religion, mischaracterised as malign witchcraft by the Christian church in order to stamp it out. Murray's theories were not initially challenged, perhaps because few historians took sufficient interest in the history of witch persecutions. A rebuttal appeared in 1963, however, and criticism snowballed. While Murray's theories were effectively discredited from the 1970s onwards, they did help support the development of the modern western practice of witchcraft, including Wicca.

The issue with Murray's theory is not the idea that pre-Christian religion existed, but rather that it persisted in organised practice. Naturally we understand that pre-Christian beliefs existed in Scotland as elsewhere, and we understand that some societies believed in pantheons of gods and goddesses versus single deities, just as various cultures do today. Shades of goddesses and other mythical women appear throughout folklore, and Gaelic folklore in particular shows a comfort with women's magic, which is not characterised as diabolical, but rather elemental. As noted elsewhere, this may go some way to explaining the relative lack of persecutions in most Gaelic strongholds.

We do know that belief in magic and practice of magic persisted after the persecutions were over. This bears no resemblance to the witch-hunters' fevered fantasies of digging up corpses and turning into hares and having sex with Satan. Rather it is the sort of magic that has probably always existed to some degree in society to give comfort when it is needed: charms for safe passage, visions obtained through 'second sight', or harmless rituals such as placing a silver coin in a cradle to keep a child from harm.

In telling Scotland's story, it is important also to remember that we are part of a greater world, have been impacted by that world, and have impacted upon it in turn. The witch panics are a dark stain on our history and they are not the only one. We are only just coming to terms with our country's role in the slave trade and as part of that many people are realising for the first time that our history includes the many people of colour who made their homes here as a result of that process, as well as the many others who have settled here through choice or necessity. Their traditions of magic may not be the same as ours.

In the pages that follow you will find three women – one fictional, one not and one halfway in between, who own their very different models of magic.

"In telling Scotland's story, it is important also to remember that we are part of a greater world, have been impacted by that world, and have impacted upon it in turn."

"No, I have never had the gift of convincing the daughters. Perhaps they recognise women's magic when they feel it, perhaps it is of them too."

LITTLE YELLOW COMB
(A' CHÌR BHUIDHE)

FOR THE EACHLAIR ÙRLAIR /
DON EACHLAIR ÙRLAIR
AND FOR THE GENERATIONS OF STORYTELLERS WHO KEPT HER NAME ALIVE

WHAT WE KNOW

I n Gaelic wonder-tales stepmothers often start out as anything but wicked. The queen is dead, the king and his children are bereft, and the new young wife takes the family to her bosom. But then the Eachlair Ùrlair arrives to pour her poison in the poor woman's ear. As Gaelic storyteller Duncan MacDonald of Peninerine says in his version of the *Three Shirts of Bog Cotton:*

> " . . then who came to the place but the Eachlair Ùrlair, and I don't really know what sort of woman she was, but she was a bad woman, and she came to many places. "

As Duncan says, the Eachlair Ùrlar is a little inscrutable. Her name appears in different configurations – the first part may be *Eachrais* ('confusion, disturbance') or *Eachlair* (literally 'ostler', deriving from *each*, 'horse'). The second part may be *Ùrlair* ('floor') or *Amhlair* ('fool'). She is always a woman, always malevolent and always a magical being, but her origins are not clear. Perhaps she is a survivor of an older tradition or a hangover of older beliefs.

Bad as she is, the Eachlair Ùrlair is not satanic. She works in the service of no greater evil; her ill will is her own. Her magic – indeed magic in general – is elemental. This cultural attitude to magic may have been one factor that guarded against characterisations of witchcraft as specifically in opposition to sacred beliefs.

READ ON FOR HOW IT MIGHT HAVE BEEN . . .

To DO WHAT I DO, I must first find the cracks in people.

A second wife, anxious, uncertain. The late queen was so lovely, so wise, so kind, and what living woman can compete for affection with the sainted dead mother? This girl will not inherit; any children she has will be thrown on the charity of the first wife's brats. She is easy meat for me.

What if the king were to die tomorrow? I whisper. *Your portion would be much smaller than the children's.*

She was a beauty, was she not, the queen? The daughter cannot bear that he loves another. She can't wait to be rid of you. Just wait till your husband dies, you'll see.

I feel for your own children. They'll get nothing, poor babes. Almost better they were never born…

Everyone has a point where they will give. With such cunning words I twist and I prise until I find the place, and at last her heart is laid open to me. Then my power feasts. It grows heavy and coiling, and there is nothing I cannot do. For form's sake I ask for payment. Seven granaries of oats, seven byres of cattle, seven folds of sheep, that sort of thing, but these are trifles, mortal wealth. All I really need is to feed my magic.

Can you imagine the triumph of turning a boy into a raven? The power it takes to compress five feet of bone, sinew, muscle and teeth into a bird no higher than my knee? To make feathers burst through skin where none grew before, a nose curve and twist until it forms a beak, toes warp and harden into claws?

It is no mean feat. The power surges upwards and outwards from my core, crackling in my fingertips, making stray strands of my hair dance in the air. Sometimes I use a wand to help channel it. It is nothing fancy; no carving, no special materials, no enchantments. I favour a simple switch of hazel: it is a pliable wood and will not crack. Sometimes I imagine I can smell it burning as the power courses through it, but it has never scorched. In any case, magic can be a smelly business. When a large body is compressed into a small one there can be … *matter* left over. And fluids emitted in fear.

Not all of my transformations are so immediately violent. I like the long game too, the subtle tricks that play with men's minds and send women frantic. Among these are those any butcher could achieve – slaughtering a favourite horse, say, or a bull, or a dog and smearing its blood on a sleeping child – but I don't mind the rougher work. Sometimes a little theatre is useful. For then there is fear, and anger, and confusion and my power can sate its hunger once more. It rises up and I can work my sleeping charms, magic my poisoned combs, unleash my pet hailstones to carry a young mother to her grave.

Distance is no barrier to my magic. The king's daughter may flee to Ireland with her lover, or to Greece, or Lochlann, but she can never outrun me. One day a box will come that bears her father's crest. She will tear it open, hungry for news of home, only to find waiting my gift of freezing death. I can tell to the minute when it has happened, for whenever a spell hits its mark, a great joy bubbles through me and I laugh and laugh until I am spent.

It is not true that my power knows no bounds. It is women's magic I have, and grown men do not often fall under my spell. Boys are fine, although the younger they are, the better it works, and the magic may be imperfect when they are nearing their maturity. Day as a raven, night as a boy – that sort of thing. It's a nuisance.

Worse, though, are the girl children. They often elude me. Although perhaps that is not a weakness in the magic, but rather in my own self. I speak in the same bright tone I use with the boys, I smile the same smiles, I spin the same small endearments.

There's the yellow comb, over there on the dresser, and over you go my little warrior-girl, and pick it up.

Hurry along now, my dear, and take the box to your stepmother. She has need of it.

Your brothers, my love? I've seen neither hide nor hair of them here today . . .

It does not work.

No, I have never had the gift of convincing the daughters. They seem to sense too much in my interest in them, an unnatural brightness in my smile, perhaps, a too-hard glitter in my eye. Or perhaps they recognise women's magic when they feel it, perhaps it is of them too.

Since I first recognised this, I have tried to stay away from the girls. Now I prefer to charge the stepmother with all dealings with the family – even the silliest chit of a girl can usually follow my orders, although often I need to repeat myself.

Tell the king you'll die unless he casts his daughter aside.

Tell him to make sure she's gone for good.

Tell him to bring you her heart and her liver . . . and her little finger.

The daughters can still surprise me. I do not have the gift of foretelling, and I cannot always see what they will do. People are unpredictable.

Part of me admires their wit. I ask myself what I would have done had my father told me my stepmother wanted him to kill me and give her my heart and my liver and my little finger as proof. I do not know if I would have been willing to cut off the dratted finger so he could give it to her along with the heart and liver of a lamb. I would certainly never have said I would feel no pain because of my father's love for me. Cutting a finger off hurts; anyone who tells you any different is lying. Besides, I wasn't that fond of my father.

It is harder to swallow the fact that the most recent one outsmarted the *geas* with which I bound her.

She may not be on foot, she may not be on horseback and she may not be on the green earth the day she tells what her stepmother and I have done, and this is a baptismal oath.

How was I to foresee the damned girl would go capering around the hall of her husband's castle balanced on the back of a boar while she whispered the secret into the ear of the child she had specifically chosen not to baptise for that very purpose?

She was a cunning one, I have to give her that.

And so I begin again, at the bottom of the sea, in the frankly dull form of a pillar of stone. My hazel rod still bore enough magic for them to strike me with it and turn my own gifts against me.

Now I must bide my time until I rise again. Power like mine cannot be tamed forever.

Queens will die, kings will mourn. New wives will chafe against their binds.

Yes, as long as there are stories to tell and Gaelic to tell them, I will return.

(DON'T) LIVE YOUR LIFE BY EACHLAIR ÙRLAIR

✸ What do you think is the appeal of the wicked witch as a character?

✸ Some film critics argue that our ideas of witches today are strongly influenced by Disney, and in creating baddies, Disney turned to Hollywood 'femme fatales'. Does this make sense to you?

✸ Is the image of an empowered 'bad woman' a positive for women?

"I know there are those who would say that what I do is wrong, for have I not lived longer than anybody deserves while I have sold my prayers to lads who have barely seen a score of years?"

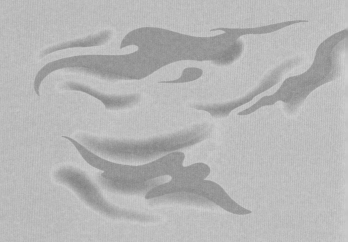

THE FAVOUR
OF THE WIND

FOR BESSIE MILLAR

WHAT WE KNOW

Bessie Millar was one of a number of women in the nineteenth century who eked out a living by taking a few pence from every sailor who wished to procure a favourable wind. Witches had long been thought to be able to raise storms, and calm them again when their work was done, and the belief persisted that there were those among the population who could do so still. As the memory of the persecutions receded, those who chose to profit from 'selling the wind' were free to do so, if at a slight risk of prosecution under the Witchcraft Act 1736 for pretending to practise magic.

We know the names of a few of the women who 'sold the wind', but Bessie is perhaps the most famous of all, since she entertained the writer and antiquarian Sir Walter Scott in her home on Brinkie's Brae in Stromness, Orkney. When Scott met Bessie she was almost one hundred years old. Scott was taken aback by Bessie's appearance, and by the 'dirty and precipitous lanes' leading to her house in Stromness. His distaste made its way into his portrayal of her in his 1822 novel *The Pirate*, where she is described in very unflattering terms.

Bessie was proud to tell Scott that she did not meddle in the sorts of tricks that others did with threads or rope tied into various knots that the sailor might loosen if the need arose. Mammie Scott, her nearest competitor, did use these, forming her creations with red thread for extra flourish (sailors were warned never to loosen the final knot, for that would unleash a hurricane). Bessie simply boiled her kettle, took her sixpence, and said a prayer.

HERE IS ANOTHER STORY; UNLIKE SCOTT'S, THIS ONE IS IN HER HONOUR . . .

W HEN THEY COME TO ME, those lads, I always make sure to take my time about getting them sat down in the big chair and making them a cup of tea. I'm still sprightly enough on my feet for a woman past four score years and ten, but I struggle to lift the kettle these days and so of course they get out of the chair to come over and help me. I say what a help they must be to their mother, if they're young, or to their wife if they're married. And if they're not married I ask them do they have a sweetheart and what's her name. And once or twice I've seen how it was and surprised a lad by asking 'what's *his* name?' instead, and they started at first but then they told me, every one of them, blushing and stammering out 'a friend from school' or 'sailed together to the Indies'. The youngest ones, I ask about their families, and how many bairns does their mother have and is their father still living.

I do what I can with my prayers, then, but half the point is to listen to what they have to tell me. I'm a God-fearing woman, and I have some skill in protection, but only what He has seen fit to give me. I cannot change His will. And so the talk over the tea is an insurance, of sorts, against the day word comes – and come it does, the sea is a cruel mistress – that this mother or that wife need not expect her dear lad home. Then I can go to that woman and tell her what he said of her to me, and how fondly he thought of the bairnies, or how his heart always longed for home. Once I went to the home of one of those young men, up by Hill of Quholm, and I told him I had heard that the Rendall lad would not be coming back. No one else had thought to send word to him, for they had not understood that he had the greatest need to know.

I can no longer manage the brae, these days, and so when there is a death I do not go myself but I send word by my nephew Thomas instead. I tell him to say Bessie Millar has bid him come with her kind wishes in their time of sorrow, and bids him tell them of the sweet words their lad spoke to her before he sailed. They sit him down, those poor wives and mothers, and ply him with tea and sweet things, for everyone in this island knows how a guest should be treated. And he tells them the words I have told him to say, about how their lad dreamed of being home again with his wages for his mother, a pipe for his father made of the wood of the mahogany tree, a shell picture for his wife who was his sweetheart still, though they were married fifteen years with three bairnies in school. He's a sweet lad, Thomas, and he listens then as they weep over their William or their Geordie, and tells them I said to say he was not afraid, he went with God, and if God has seen fit to take him for now, then they will surely meet again in the hereafter.

Thomas will inherit this house when I am gone and I hope he thrives here, and marries and has bairns of his own. He will make a fine man for some girl, only I hope he never goes to sea.

I know there are those who would say that what I do is wrong, that I am a foolish old woman to carry on so, and a shameless one forby, for have I not lived longer than anybody deserves while I have sold my prayers to lads who have barely seen a score of years? Let them say so if they wish, it does not worry me. If God is not pleased with me then I will answer to Him on the Day of Judgement, and I will tell Him that every blessing I ever put on a lad was no more than a prayer, to send him on his way strong of faith and stout of heart.

LIVE YOUR LIFE BY BESSIE

* Do you believe in any elements of the supernatural?

* Bessie seems not to have seen any conflict between her Christian faith and taking money for luck. Do you see any conflict?

* What do you think prompted Bessie to offer the service she did?

"A skin of oil might vanish from the Big House kitchen to make healing rubs or tonics, a rag might suffice to make a pouch of protection, or a handful of flour stuffed into an apron pocket might form the basis of a powder to keep Ole Higue at bay."

CORP-CRÈADHA
(FIGURE OF CLAY)

FOR DOLL

WHAT WE KNOW

A woman known as Doll lived with the family of Lieutenant Soirle (Sorley) MacDonald of Skye. We know of her because MacDonald received a letter in 1782 from high command at the Brigade, New York, giving him permission to take Doll on campaign during the American War of Independence. No human being should ever 'belong' to another, but Doll was enslaved and under the unjust system of the time she was the property of MacDonald's daughter Mary. The letter concerning her is held today in the JLM Mitchell Archive of the Gaelic Society of Inverness.

MacDonald was originally from Skye, but in 1771 he emigrated with his family to North Carolina, just one family among thousands to leave the Highlands as the Clearances undermined traditional Gaelic society. Doll was probably born in America, but in the story that follows she has a different backstory. This is intended to acknowledge the presence in the Highlands in the 1700s and 1800s of a significant African population, both enslaved and free, brought from the Caribbean by Highland Scots returning from slave-worked plantations. Many of these people were the children of Highland men, born to enslaved and to 'free coloured' women. Their story has been neglected in Highland history, as involvement in slavery has more generally been neglected in Scotland's broader story.

In this story Doll is therefore born in Jamaica and is acquainted with Obeah, a set of spiritual practices which include – but are not limited to – those that correspond with Western ideas of 'magic'. Obeah encompasses healing, justice-making and more. In this way it relates rather more to the Gaelic concept of magic than to the Lowland Scottish and broader European equivalents. Takyi ('Tacky') and Queen Nanny ('Nanny of the Maroons') were real people, attested in the record. Both are credited with having used Obeah to inspire their followers. All the women Doll remembers in her first home are fictional; they have Akan and Igbo names as – while we do not know the origins of many slaves in Jamaica, we do know that both of these peoples were affected. Akan people would have been brought to Jamaica from present-day Ghana and Ivory Coast and Igbo people from present-day Nigeria.

HOW IT MIGHT HAVE BEEN . . .

DOLL FINDS THE MANNIKIN as she goes about her work in the upper floor of the house. It is made of wax and is vaguely human-shaped, and there is a gingerish lock of hair stuck into one side of it that looks like the master's. It has a pin thrust deep into the place between its legs.

Doll's smile almost becomes a laugh at the sight, but she catches herself in time and closes her lips over her teeth. The master is well known for being free with his hands; he steers clear of Doll but few other women escape his attentions. She tucks the little model back under the pile of freshly-laundered linen where she found it, wondering who has taken it into their head to try a little magic.

It has been years since Doll herself last thought of such things. She was a little over seven when they took her from the shack where she lived with her mother and the other women in the fields, and carried her struggling and protesting to the house. There they stripped and deloused her and burned her clothes before her eyes. The fight went out of her then, watching every single thing that was her own go up in smoke. It seems to her now that she left a part of her first self there in the ashes with the remains of her cotton smock. In place of the smock came skirts and bodices and complicated underpinnings, constricting and heavy so Doll sweated and itched in the heat and had her hand smacked purple for scratching. Those were the least of the beatings; scarce an inch of her remained unbruised as she moved through the first clumsy steps of her new life, dancing attendance on the niece of the overseer's wife. This Miss Mary was a girl of her own age, a puny creature paler and more fragile even than the china poppet that was her most cherished possession. Of course she called her new slave Doll, and continues to call her Doll, for all they are women grown, and have been for years.

Effia, Doll whispers to herself. She has not spoken this, her real name, aloud for almost twenty years. Three small syllables, but so much lies within them. Grief for her long-lost mother and the other women, their fates unknown to her and never to be known to her, in this life at least. A feeling of being adrift, four thousand miles and half a lifetime away from her very self. And there is a small spark of rebellion, too, flaring through the damp grey numbness of life in this place that is not her own.

Alone in the peat-smoke dark of the room where she sleeps, Doll at last allows herself to open the door she has kept firmly bolted for a dozen and more years and step into the past. On the other side she tiptoes into the breathing dark of the shack in the fields where she was begun. She passes the mat where her mother sleeps, her mouth open, worn out from a day's hard toil in the fields. Next to her mother is a woman whose name Doll cannot at first remember, but then it returns to her. *Yaaba*. She was an old woman, or seemed old, but she was wiry and strong, and they whipped her once for demanding the doctor attend a sick child after she had twice been told he would not come. Yaaba is cuddled into Doll's mother's side like a child, or perhaps a lover, her left hand cradling Madda's breast. There is a guard ring on her index finger, a fragile twist of grass she trusts to keep her from ill.

Doll pauses a moment to blink back tears – Yaaba is likely dead now, she knows, Madda too perhaps – before she walks on. Her memory self picks her way carefully between the sleeping bodies – Ugochukwu, she remembers, and her daughter Chibundo, the next youngest to herself – until she reaches the place nearest the door where two women whisper and murmur, their heads bent together and their hands busy with some task she cannot see. One is Akua, who lives here in the shack, the other a stranger. A third sits with her back against the jamb of the door, almost invisible in the shadows but for the glint of her eyes. She is keeping watch, making sure no one can approach the shack and witness the transaction taking place inside. For Akua is an Obeah Woman, a purveyor of talismans to secure love and blessings, amulets to block harm.

Obeah was illegal in Jamaica then, and Doll imagines it is still, because Obeah gives believers hope and hope is a dangerous thing when a small group of men wish to keep a multitude in fear. Queen Nanny used her powers to stand firm for years against the colonists in the heart of the island, at last bending them to her will so they signed over to her the freedom of her village and her people. Doll was still in Jamaica when the slave named Takyi rose up with five hundred and more followers across the island. Takyi was no slave truly seen, of course (*For who is a slave truly seen?*) but a great king and a warlord in his homelands, and he had a fierce band of Obeah Men with him. They say the Obeah Men gave the fighters a powder that would render them immortal under the storm of the white men's bullets. Those fighters believed an Obeah Man could never be killed, really believed it, and at the end the planters' soldiers took to slaughtering the Obeah Men and stringing them up with their masks and bottles and talismans, in the hope that in this way they might break the spirits of Takyi's men.

That was when Miss Mary had told Doll her father was taking her away from the dangers of Jamaica and home to Skye. Doll spoke English then but not brilliantly, and her first, stupid thought was that Miss Mary was somehow going to live in the heavens. On a cloud, perhaps, although Doll could not see how such a thing could be possible. She had not expected that she would go too, thinking with a leaping heart of how pleased Madda would be by her return, at long last, to the shack. But Miss Mary was not to be parted from her treasures. The china poppet, her little dog and her Black slave were all to be packed up and shipped off home with her. Doll would find out that Skye was a place on Earth, an island in Scotland, although it did almost seem they dwelled in the clouds sometimes, so misty and rainy and damp and cold did the place turn out to be.

But the dream shack where Doll still stands exists in a time before all that, when Takyi's war was no more than whisperings in a cave, or perhaps Takyi was even back home in Africa still, making war against other people, yes, but fairly, following rules laid down generations before.

Akua still risked a whipping if she was caught practising Obeah, hence the lookout. But still the believers came and somehow, even in this poor shack, Akua managed to come by the necessary ingredients and implements to ply her trade. A skin of oil might vanish from the Big House kitchen to make healing rubs or tonics, a rag might suffice to make a pouch of protection, or a handful of flour stuffed into an apron pocket might form the basis of a powder to keep Ole Higue at bay so that a babe might be born without killing its mother, and moreover might thrive. There was a particular fear of duppies, the shadows of men and women that may be left behind when the person dies. Many rituals were recommended, many pouches made up of earth and hair or blood or nail clippings, to ensure the duppy could not cause evil or mischief to the living.

Doll wonders now if she is a duppy of sorts, a shadow of a woman moving silently in dark corners, stepping on and on as if unaware that her heart is stopped, her soul gone and really she is dead. But then she decides not, the real duppy is surely Miss Mary, a woman without a heart, without work, without a purpose but to acquire trinkets and possessions, up to and including the human kind.

Doll closes the door to the memory shack and decides she will begin her resistance against Miss Mary with the dawn. She will make her own pouch and will fill it with ease, for which of Mary's bodily leavings are private from Doll? Who else cuts her toenails, trims her hair, empties her shit from the night pot and wrings out her bloody napkins each full moon? One of Mary's kidskin gloves will do to sew the pouch itself and she will moan and bewail its loss while Doll pretends to search, asks where she wore it last, did she not come bare-handed into the house last week, for she stopped to pick a posy of wildflowers on the way from church? Perhaps she dropped it then . . .

They are to travel to America soon, Miss Mary says, where the master may soon be called again to fight in yet another white man's war. There are thousands and thousands and thousands of slaves in that land, Doll knows, and where there are slaves there are murmurings and whisperings and plans for freedom. Miss Mary may yet live to regret taking Doll from this prison on Skye to a place where she will again find her own kind, and perhaps, just perhaps, she will find a way to shape a new self from the healing beliefs of her people.

LIVE YOUR LIFE BY DOLL

✴ In terms of your own life and education, were you taught about Scotland's involvement in the slave trade?

✴ Why do you think the history of people from minority ethnic backgrounds in Scotland has been neglected to date?

✴ What do you think about the 'decolonisation' of Scotland's public realm (for example the renaming of streets and buildings or removal of statues)?

TENDING THE FLAME: REMEMBERING SCOTLAND'S WITCHES

SCOTLAND HAS NO NATIONAL memorial to its witches. Several individual communities do, however, mark the victims.

In several communities, memorials are single stones or cairns erected at various points in time. There are examples in Forres, Bo'ness, Dunning in Perthshire and Spott in East Lothian. The Forfar one is brilliantly to the point, reading 'The Forfar Witches: Just People'. A stone in Dornoch marks the place where Janet Horne was executed, the last person to die under the Witchcraft Act. Other stones exist that are said to mark the place of execution of local witches but the details have been forgotten (details are also unverified in the case of examples such as the Dunning memorial).

The 1894 Witches' Well in Edinburgh has been joined by a number of newer commissioned pieces – and thankfully these recognise injustice in all cases. In Dundee, there is a mosaic set into the ground in Peter Street to mark the place where Grissel Jaffray was executed in 1669. A brass plaque at Maxwellton Cross in Paisley reads 'Pain Inflicted, Suffering Endured, Injustice Done' and memorialises seven people burned at the Gallow Green in 1696. In Culross in Fife a plaque memorialises all Fife witches as 'Innocent victims of unenlightened times'. A mural in Aberdeen outside St Nicholas Church, where the accused were imprisoned, gives significant detail about the persecutions. An unusual memorial exists in Crook of Devon. It is a beech maze at Tullibole Castle, in the centre of which stands a pillar memorialising eleven victims killed in 1662. A plaque in Kirkwall repeats the simple message of the Forfar Stone in Orcadian: 'They wur cheust folk.'

All across Scotland statues of women are rare: Edinburgh has more statues of named animals than it does of its women. As this imbalance has entered the public consciousness, there has been an uplift in efforts both to memorialise women and to do so through statues as well as plaques and other smaller pieces of street art. East Lothian has set about righting this wrong with enthusiasm, erecting in recent years both a statue to Jackie Crookston, heroine of the Massacre of Tranent, and a woman's figure erected in Prestonpans to commemorate the eighty-one people from that community who died in the witch persecutions.

While not a 'memorial' in the traditional sense, it would be wrong to discuss the ways in which we remember Scotland's witches without referencing the incredible work of the historians, researchers and others who have discovered and publicised their stories. The killing of Katherine MacKinnon, for example, was uncovered by Skye archivist Catherine MacPhee. Of particular importance in this context is the Survey of Scottish Witchcraft, which stands as a memorial to the witches in its own right. Julian Goodare, Lauren Martin, Joyce Miller and Louise Yeoman conceived of this idea in the late 1990s in what is now the School of History, Classics and Archaeology at Edinburgh University. The group recognised that they could not only collate and add to the range of information available about known witches, but also that additional witches were in the records to be found. The Survey database holds as much data as the team could locate relating to the accused, their denunciation, investigation and, where relevant, their trials and executions. In 2019, this data underpinned another Edinburgh University project to geolocate Scotland's witches, resulting in a brilliantly useful interactive map that has contributed hugely to public understanding of the persecutions.

Witches of Scotland campaign for a national memorial such as the Steilneset Memorial in Vardø in north-east Norway. There is a popular view that one possible site may be Torryburn in Fife, since Torryburn Bay is the site of the only known grave of a 'witch' in Scotland. This is the burial place of Lilias Adie.

"They wur cheust folk."
(They were just people)

MEMORIAL STONE, KIRKWALL

"They must work under cover of darkness, for there are still plenty in this village who would say that a witch's grave should not be disturbed. That's why her accusers laid her remains here under half a ton of stone, after all – so she could not rise again to do the Devil's work on Earth."

POINTING THE FINGER

FOR LILIAS ADIE

WHAT WE KNOW

Lilias (or Lilly) Adie was accused of witchcraft in 1704 by a neighbour, when she was around sixty years of age. The local minister was an enthusiastic persecutor of witches and under his auspices Lilias was imprisoned and interrogated over a period of more than a month. She eventually confessed to having submitted to the Devil and having had sexual relations with him. Her confession was probably made under torture but despite her sufferings she did not implicate any other women, with the exception of neighbours who had already been accused of witchcraft and women who were already dead.

Had she been tried and convicted, Lilias would have been strangled and her body burned. She escaped this fate only because she died before a trial could happen. It was unusual for the authorities to be in possession of the body of a witch – the point of burning witches was to ensure they could not be used after death as a vessel for satanic activity – and they decided on a symbolic disposal of Lilias's remains. She was buried between the high and low tide marks in the bay at Torryburn, in a simple wooden box under an enormous slab of stone.

In 1852 Lilias's body was exhumed by curio-hunters who supplied her coffin and partial remains to Joseph Paton, a Fife artist, antiquary and folklorist. Paton exhibited her skull in his private museum before it passed to a local doctor and then St Andrews University Museum. The wood of the coffin (or purportedly of the coffin) was made into souvenirs. These included a walking stick gifted to the industrialist Andrew Carnegie.

Lilias's skull was exhibited at the Empire Exhibition in Glasgow in the 1930s, the last point at which its whereabouts are known.

In 2017 a team of forensic artists at the University of Dundee reconstructed her face from photographs of the skull taken in the early 1900s. Subsequent interest in Lilias's story led to Fife Council launching an appeal to locate her remains for burial, and to call for a memorial to Scotland's witches near her grave at Torryburn.

In the following pages you will find a story of Lilias, her treatment, and the treatment of her remains. Like the others it is fictionalised, but unlike the others it has no questions for you to ponder and rather is written to stand alone.

The story in this book is for Lilias and all of her fellow 'witches'. They were just folk, and their treatment is to our country's shame. Let's hope they can be properly memorialised, and for now may this book be a stone on their cairn.

HOW IT MIGHT HAVE BEEN . . .

THE MUSEUM

IT IS NOT A LARGE museum, but it was founded by a philanthropist in the Victorian era and in common with many other institutions of its vintage, the Riverlee holds in its collection objects that are sensitive in nature. Some are items sacred to other people and places, amulets, clothing or weaponry that may not be sold or given. These carry within their very fabric a way of looking at the world, a stock of belief and belonging, an echo of a language or a song. 'Donated' to the Riverlee by colonial administrators, army officers or missionaries, it is impossible to say whether any individual item was stolen, looted or more or less fairly acquired as the colonial project reduced to baubles the living heritage of the oppressed.

The Riverlee has begun the process of decolonisation. In this it is led by its Curator of Material Culture, Dr Alice James. Alice believes in repatriating sacred objects and reinterpreting those which might reasonably be held outside the communities within which they originate – a task she undertakes in partnership with said communities. Moreover, Alice believes that the status quo must be challenged in the museums sector, structures rethought. Until people from originating communities are actually working in museums permanently and for the long term, there will never be true institutional change.

Alice does not enjoy the full support of her colleagues. Malcolm, the Director, has apparently photographic recall of policy statements and can be relied upon to cite the position of the most useful professional association at the drop of a hat. Repatriation is a 'complex issue involving a range of emotional, ethical, legal and political factors,' he parrots, with an earnest smile.

Malcolm is currently stalling on the removal or reinterpretation of human remains in the collection. Among some five-hundred-plus holdings are a 'shrunken head' from the Achuar people in Ecuador, a mummified Egyptian woman and a range of skeletal remains from across the globe. Malcolm cites a recent survey to the effect that only nine per cent of people oppose the display of human bones in museums. This, he says, supports his own belief that the educational benefits of learning from human remains outweigh the rights of the dead. Display of human remains can greatly stimulate empathy, he argues, allowing a much stronger connection to the culture that is being represented.

Alice believes that the displays in the Riverlee more often suggest human beings from other cultures to be 'savage', 'primitive' or gruesome. For now, though, she chooses to focus on her own scheme of redress and repatriation and tackle Malcolm again at a later date.

And so the woman's finger bone remains on show in its case, beside its discredited 'reliquary', unchampioned by Alice or anyone else. It was carbon dated during some previous period of plentiful funding and identified as Early Modern. Had Alice thought about that, and the crushing injury to the finger, the little digit might have sparked a line of thought as to the hypocrisy of cultures that view others as savage. It might even have led to the finger being reunited with the rest of its body, or at least what is left of it. But Alice must choose her battles, and so she does, and children continue to peer into the case and say 'yuck' and shudder, then laugh and run on to look at the headsman's axe and the penis of a whale.

THE DEALER

Thaddeus Crawford is experiencing a bad week for business. In fact, he is experiencing a bad month in a succession of months sufficiently poor as to constitute a bad year. He is not minded to dwell on this thought, however, for thus far he has managed to satisfy his creditors, pay his late mother's charwoman to make his meals and procure fuel for the stove on colder nights.

Tonight the room behind the showroom has just reached a comfortable temperature and Jean has dropped off a pigeon pie to which he is settling down when there is a knock on the shop door. He opens the door a crack to conserve the heat and is required to adjust his gaze rapidly downwards to where a dirty urchin is thrusting a grubby parcel towards him.

'I've got a relict for ye,' the boy says. 'It's a finger. Six shillings.'

Thaddeus stifles a laugh.

'A *relict* is a widow,' he says, not unkindly. 'A dead man's wife. A relic is the bone of a saint. But I don't imagine that's what you have. It's probably a meat bone. I can't give you anything for it.'

'No it isnae,' the boy insists. 'It's human. A wifie's finger. Six shillings.'

Thaddeus considers shutting the door but something in him is tickled by the audacious approach.

'One shilling,' he says, aware this is no more or less than charitable giving.

'Three,' says the boy.

'One,' says Thaddeus again, 'and a slice of bread and gravy.'

The boy weighs up this offer for a moment and then gives a curt nod. He hops from foot to foot at the door while Thaddeus cuts a slice of bread and dips it in the gravy of the pie. At the last moment he cuts a second slice and adds an apple to the bounty.

When the boy has disappeared into the drizzly Dundee dark with his coin and bread, Thaddeus sits down to his own meal. He finishes the pie, lights his pipe and turns to the grubby bundle on the table by his plate.

Once unwrapped, Thaddeus is surprised to see that the bone within does, indeed, appear to be human. It is an index finger, he thinks, small and delicate, but with some damage, as though it has been crushed. His first, disgusted thought is that the digit has been lost by someone in the boy's family in an accident but then he looks again and decides that the bone is of some apparent antiquity, yellowed with age. Perhaps it has been dug from a grave, or perhaps it really is a saint's relic, liberated in some past time from a long-forgotten monastery or convent. He hopes it is not part of the remains of a murder victim.

As he dons his nightgown, Thaddeus recalls an article he read last week about the founding of a museum in the city. A saint's relic might fetch a fair price from the curators there, he thinks. Somewhere he has a book of Scottish saints he read as a boy; was not Margaret of Wessex dug up from before the altar in Dunfermline and distributed in pieces around the Continent? Thaddeus blows out the candle and begins to plan the procurement of an appropriate vessel for a 'Spanish relic', traded home to Scotland and lost for the best part of three hundred years.

The Pearl of Scotland, he thinks as he drifts off, *that's what they called Saint Margaret*. Her finger will pay for pigeon pies for some time to come.

THE BOOT BOY

Alex is a footman, a second footman to be precise. He is four years David's senior and two times his superior in the hierarchy of the household, and he will not let David forget this. He never misses a chance to stick his foot out as David passes with his box of brushes and polish, or to smear mud on a newly-cleaned pair of brogues.

David is lonely without his brothers and sisters, and perhaps that's why he lets his guard down when Alex suddenly starts to be nice. First he gives him a boiled sweet, the first such treat David has ever tasted in his short and hungry life. Next he helps him shovel a pile of coal into the bunker. Then he offers to take David to see His Lordship's new carriage in the coach house.

That's where the thing happens that David does not understand, but knows at the heart of him to be darker and more wrong than any of the myriad depredations to which he has been subject in his short life. The men do things to him that hurt and mess him, and Alex stands in the shadow of the carriage and watches. David understands that they have done these things to Alex too, and sees in the hard glitter of the older boy's eyes that he has traded a new victim for his own freedom.

After three months of it, David decides he must run away. He knows he cannot go home; his mother can barely feed the others with the paltry wages he sends her, let alone manage with no money and David to feed as well. He must make his own way in the world, somehow. Perhaps he can get to the mills across the Tay, if he can find the money for the boat.

That's when David decides to steal whatever he can before he goes. It is not easy, for he has little access to the house beyond the boot room, the scullery and the stables. He begins to stow away small items of food here and there, a pair of stirrups from the tack room, a set of bootlaces, a tin of polish, some dice. No one misses these things, cheap, old and worn down as they are. Then one evening the first footman asks him to help the housemaid carry out the ashes from the library. While her back is turned, he grabs a handful of things from a desk at random, without looking, and stuffs them in his trousers. Back in his room he turns out his pockets, hoping for a gold pen or an ivory-handled knife. But all he has is rubbish – a pencil and an old bone, one of the 'curiosities' the housemaid moans about dusting. Gives her the creepings, she says, but the housekeeper says rich folk like His Lordship find interest in such things, the bones of saints from the olden times and suchlike dirt.

Now David has stolen these useless articles he knows he has no choice but to go. He stuffs his food supplies, the stirrups, the dice and the polish in his pockets with the pencil and the bone, and lights out towards the coach house. When he is out of sight of the back door he takes to his heels and pelts into the dark.

THE COLLECTOR

Oxley-Hope fancies himself an intellectual, and at first he is delighted by the invitation to join Thorne and the others in what they rather grandly style an 'invisible college'. He has visions of evenings in the library debating Boole's latest paper on logic or Ruskin's theories of architecture with like-minded gentlemen.

In fact the club has little in common with those seventeenth-century groupings from which it takes its name, unless the aim of the alchemists and intelligencers of old was to pass around dirty pictures and exchange tips on horses. Oxley-Hope is interested in neither, but these are his neighbours and there is little other society here to speak of, and so he continues to have Thomson lay out his evening dress on the last Thursday of each month and have the coach readied for the drive to whichever great house is hosting them on this occasion.

Tonight, when he is shown into Thorne's library, he is surprised to see the room has been transformed into something more akin to the place of study he had first imagined. The great table is set with an odd collection of objects – wood, bones, dark piles of what might once have been fabric. More wood is strewn upon the floor.

'Oxley-Hope!' bellows Thorne, his face flushed with brandy. 'Meet Paton. Painter, you know.'

The painter is a young man, curly-haired, serious of countenance. He bows. Oxley-Hope is suddenly shy. He nods curtly and walks over to the table.

'What's all this, then?' he asks.

'The bones of a witch,' the painter says. 'At least, a woman accused of witchcraft. Some local lads dug her up and they brought her to me.'

'Why?' Oxley-Hope asks. He can't see the link with painting.

'I'm known to have an interest in such things,' the painter says. 'Well, in tales and songs and the history folk in these parts tell each other.'

There is a guffaw from the other side of the room. Oxley-Hope looks over and sees Rogerson miming something unspeakable with the woman's skull while Thorne and Laidlaw cheer him on. Paton pretends not to notice.

Oxley-Hope does his best to block the view as he turns back to the table. 'How did she die?' he asks. 'When?'

'Just after the turn of the eighteenth century,' Paton says. 'It's hard to say how. She wasn't put to death; if she had been, the body would have been burned. She supposedly died under interrogation. She was a good age and they must have tortured her – see, one of the fingers is broken. I'm looking in the kirk session papers but I haven't found anything yet. They dealt with witchcraft locally, you see. The local minister, and the landlord – the important men in the community.'

Just then Thorne comes over.

'What d'you reckon, old chap?' he says, clapping Oxley-Hope on the shoulder. 'Paton's going to give me part of the coffin to make a walking stick. Who knows, a rap with that might bewitch that Arabian of mine into finally winning something!' He chortles at his own wit. 'You should buy a piece of it too,' he says, when he has recovered. 'Paton'll see you right. Here—' He picks up the broken finger bone and puts it into into Oxley-Hope's waistcoat pocket so the tip of the digit sticks out. 'Capital!' he roars. He claps Oxley-Hope again a couple of times on the back and wanders over to rejoin the others.

Oxley-Hope stirs at the mess on the table with his own stick. The fabric is filthy with age and whatever unthinkable substances have leached into it, but it is clear enough that it was always poor, a rough homespun.

'This is just some village wretch,' he says to Paton. 'How could they have convinced themselves that poor old women were in league with the Devil?'

Paton pauses for a second before he answers. 'I don't think they ever believed it,' he says. 'But they were rich, and they had power, and they wanted to stay rich, and keep that power. And to do that . . . well, they had to keep the poor in fear, in case they took it into their heads to ask what gives one man the right to rule over another, regardless of skill or talent or superiority of mind.' He glances over at Thorne for a moment and then turns his cool gaze back to Oxley-Hope.

Oxley-Hope feels his cheeks flush red.

'How much for the finger bone?' he asks.

'Keep it,' says Paton. 'A gift to remember this evening by.'

'Thank you,' says Oxley-Hope, awkwardly. He is uncomfortable now in the painter's company. He gives a nod and walks over to join Thorne and the others, glad for once to talk of hunting and horses.

THE GRAVE-ROBBER

The enormous slab lies on the foreshore, exposed for a few hours twice each day when the tide is out, covered in weed and shells. It is rectangular in shape, and cut from sandstone, different from the natural rocks elsewhere in the bay.

The stone has an iron ring in it and the cousins have brought ropes and horses, spades and picks to raise it. It is dirty, exhausting work, slipping and sliding and struggling for purchase in mud and salt-water. They must work under cover of darkness, for there are still plenty in this village who would say that a witch's grave should not be disturbed. That's why her accusers laid her remains here under half a ton of stone, after all – so she could not rise again to do the Devil's work on Earth.

James has dreamed of the witch every night for a week, rearing up with an angry light in her milky-white eyes and seaweed in her hair to chase them from the place where they have disturbed her rest of eight score years. Allan said James was too young to be trusted but Iain and Donald said they needed all the help they could get; the three of them and their cousins John and Malcolm are strong enough but five is barely enough for the task. And so here James is, torn between excitement and apprehension, not yet ten years old and robbing a grave.

James's task is to hold the lantern, shading it as best he can with his body so as to light the work without alerting the sleeping villagers. They have a buyer for the bones when they find them, a painter who believes the shape of a skull determines the nature of a person.

The first attempt to lift the stone fails; there is more digging and a second attempt, but still it will not budge. On the third effort the men join the straining horses on the ropes and at last there is a sucking noise and a grinding, and slowly the great stone rises.

The smell is like nothing on Earth. It is mud and rot and fish and decay and something that might be the stink of Hell. Caught by surprise, James pukes on his own feet. Allan shoots him a venomous look.

While Iain, John and Malcolm hold the stone on its edge, Allan and Donald scrabble in the mud to expose a great wooden box, longer than any of them are tall. It seems to be whole but, as they lift it out, it crumbles and a jumble of bones tip out and splash back into the water. Allan beckons to James to come closer and in the beam of the light he fishes in the water for the remains. The tide is coming in now and they open the box and tip the contents into sacks, bundling up the wooden planks that have broken off into piles. Then they drop the stone with an almighty splash, and James puts out the lantern and they return to dry land with their booty in the moonlight.

James will remember the escapade for the rest of his life. The money they got was paltry and went fast enough, as money does, and Allan and Iain and Donald went back to the fishing. They all three drowned together when their boat sank in a storm. Allan washed up in Torryburn by the witch's grave; the others were never found. John and Malcolm were also claimed by the sea, having each travelled halfway across the world in opposite directions.

James has never stopped dreaming of the witch.

THE WITCH

Lilias's pain has been worsening in the last hours. They broke her finger yesterday and now she feels every heartbeat as a twin throb, red and black and hot in her hand, and silver and sharp under the bones of her breast.

Now she has confessed, they have left her in the dark to sleep, but the pain prevents her from taking her rest, even after all the long weeks of being wrenched awake scarcely moments after her eyes could finally close.

At least she has given them no further names. She is proud of her wit, telling them only of women long dead and others she met while they were masked, like gentlewomen at a ball. They were frustrated, of course, the minister and the elders, but she gave them plenty else to keep their minds busy, the dirty sots. She made up a ceremony the Devil used to make her his own, with a hand on her feet and another on her head – that made them boggle, for she is taller than most men in the village. She said he had carnal knowledge of her, wearing a straw hat of all things – that detail came out in a delirium and she had to work not to laugh – with cold, black skin and cloven hooves. She thought back to her girlhood and told them she danced with the Devil in the moonlight at the Barnrods at Martinmas, but all the others there were dead now, and that was the truth, for that dance was fifty years in the past and not one who stood up there still living. She talked of women already burned as witches long syne, for nothing can harm them further now, poor Grissel Anderson and Euphan Stirt and the others. She did name Agnes Currie, but Agnes has been accused of witchcraft many times before and has never paid any price for it.

If she was a witch, Lilias wonders, would the Devil help her now? Her life has had few comforts and now it seems it will end at the hands of the hangman, who will squeeze the life from her before her body is burned and her ashes scattered to the wind. She hates the thought of that, dying under a man's hands while everyone she knows on Earth looks on and does nothing to aid her.

But the hangman will be robbed of his victim this time. The pain is fanning out from Lilias's breast now, into her neck and her shoulder where it tightens like a vice. She can no longer feel the pain in her hand, and her lips are numb.

Who knows whether God or the Devil has listened? Lilias Adie's suffering is past.

"How could they have convinced themselves that those poor old women were in league with the Devil?"

"I don't think they ever believed it. But they had power, and they wanted to keep that power."

HEAL AND HARROW

This book came about as part of a project by musicians Lauren MacColl and Rachel Newton to commemorate Scotland's witches. Lauren and Rachel commissioned me to produce ten stories which they used as a jumping-off point for composing the remarkable music on their album *Heal and Harrow*. You can find the music at healandharrow.com, where you can also hear some of the stories from this book read by some of the best female voice artists in Scotland. The music draws from the rich tapestry of Scottish traditional music, and the audio stories offer a precious chance to hear the women's stories in voices from the places where they lived.

MEN CHARGED WITH WITCHCRAFT

While this book focuses on associations between women and the occult, men were also accused of witchcraft, although in significantly lower numbers. The Survey of Scottish Witchcraft identifies 468 named accused men. In common with accused women, details are very limited for most cases. The following are just a few of the cases for which relatively plentiful information exists.

Alexander Drummond, Auchterarder. Drummond was a healer and confident of his powers; he claimed he could heal anyone who had not yet actually died. He directly challenged the Church, claiming his powers were greater than those of ministers, and was accused of witchcraft on the basis of claims both of his possessing a familiar spirit and of his mother having given him over to the Devil. Drummond had popular support in his home area and after his initial arrest was transferred ultimately to Edinburgh. He was strangled and burned in 1629. A later campaign sought to secure a pardon for 'ane notable Christian', claiming all of his cures were affected 'by lawfull meanes'.

Dr John Fian aka John Cunninghame, Prestonpans. Dr Fian was a schoolmaster accused of involvement in the large-scale North Berwick case of 1590–91. He made a range of odd confessions and demonstrated his abilities (some of his feats as described are suggestive perhaps of hypnotism). He recanted his supposed vows to Satan, thereafter escaping from jail. He was recaptured and grievously tortured, at which point he was reported to have denied his earlier confessions. He was strangled and burned in 1591. Dr Fian appears in this book in the story 'Bindings'.

Francis Stuart, 5th Earl of Bothwell. Francis Stuart was initially accused of treason, having led a band of 'broken men and borderers' against his cousin King James VI. Charges of necromancy and witchcraft were later added, and Bothwell was linked to the North Berwick trials. The accusation was that he had consulted with the 'witches' to help bring about the death of the king. Bothwell was held in Edinburgh Castle but escaped and was outlawed. Pursuits and counter-attacks ensued on both sides, until James pardoned Francis in 1593. A 'trial' was held to dismiss the witchcraft accusations in the same year. James reneged on the terms of the pardon almost immediately and Bothwell again rebelled. He died in relative poverty in exile in Italy in 1612. He is referenced in this book in 'Bindings'.

Major Thomas Weir, Edinburgh. Thomas Weir was not tried for witchcraft but he is listed in the Survey of Scottish Witchcraft database because of the supernatural elements of his case; the idea that he was executed for witchcraft persists into the present day. Weir was a laird's son, a soldier and a Covenanter known for his religious observance. At the age of seventy he fell ill and made a series of lurid confessions detailing incest, bestiality and fornication with various married women. His sister Jean subsequently made her own confessions of incest and of dealings with fairies and with the Devil. Jean Weir claimed her brother's stick – carved with a human head – was a magical staff from the Devil, and that the Weirs had travelled in a fiery coach to Dalkeith to meet Satan there. At his trial Weir claimed to have lain with the Devil in female guise. Thomas Weir was strangled and burned (along with his staff) and Jean hanged in 1670.

John Welch, Haddington. John Welch was from a poor family and under the age of majority when he was investigated for witchcraft in 1662. He confessed to attending over a dozen meetings of witches in various locations, of which he gave various details. He said that his mother and grandmother had taken him to meet the Devil, who had supposedly marked his thigh, and that he had seen fairy folk both male and female. Although Welch was too young to stand trial, he was imprisoned. He named around ninety other 'witches' and a number were investigated on the basis of his evidence.

SCOTTISH WITCHES TO DISCOVER IN FICTION

Marian Isbister
'Witch' in **A Calendar of Love** by George Mackay Brown
A young Orcadian woman is accused and tried for witchcraft in a process that brings community tensions to the surface.

Janet M'Clour
'Thrawn Janet' by Robert Louis Stevenson (in various anthologies)
A young minister defends his housekeeper from accusations of witchcraft and experiences a range of terrifying phenomena after he makes the woman renounce the Devil.

Minty and Jinnot
'Thou shalt not suffer a witch' in **Thou Shalt Not Suffer a Witch and other stories** by Dorothy K. Haynes
A young girl is persuaded to make an accusation of witchcraft against the serving woman who has raised her, and begins to suffer apparently real effects.

Thomas Weir
The Fanatic by James Robertson
A guide on an Edinburgh ghost tour dives into the life of the character he plays – Major Weir, executed in 1670 and associated with witchcraft ever since – and that of a seventeenth-century would-be assassin from the same religious tradition.

Various inhabitants of Woodlee
Witch Wood by John Buchan
During the Wars of the Three Kingdoms and in a plague year, a young minister discovers a witch cult in his parish.

Geillis Duncan
Hex by Jenni Fagan
A fictionalised account of Geillis Duncan's last night on earth, during which she meets an apparent traveller from another time.

NOTES

TANSY AND RUE

The quotation from the Book of Numbers in this story is from the King James Bible. This version of the Bible did not yet exist when Margerat died but is used here for ease for the modern reader.

DA DIM

The characters in the story use Shetlandic, but at the time it is set people in Foula may rather have used Norn. Midder (Mother) and Ingrid knit; this makes them very early adopters of this craft, although there were Norse weaving techniques that produced a sort of knitted result.

JUDGE NOT

Christian calls Scottish Gaelic 'Erse' ('Irish') which was common in Lowland discourse at the time. Scottish Gaelic and Irish are closely related but evolved quite differently over many hundreds of years.

GLOSSARY
(BY STORY)

TANSY AND RUE

Guid – good
Thole – bear, suffer
Sumph – stupid or sulky person
Deave – confuse, deafen, worry at

DA DIM

Skeo – a dry-stone hut
Black Patie – Patrick Stewart, 2nd Earl of Orkney
Bere – a form of barley
Johnsmas - midsummer
Heidiecra – head-over-heels
Kishie – a basket or creel
A deuk glyin for thunder – a duck squinting for thunder
Uthaleland – arable land in a township as recorded in historic valuation rolls
Brönnie – a thick oatmeal scone
Peerie – little
Dwam – daydream
Hippin – nappy
Blyde – blithe, happy
Kyoderin – caressing

SORROW AND SIGH AND MEIKLE CARE
Meikle – large, great
Puddock – a toad or a frog

BINDINGS
Kist – a wooden chest or trunk

BEHIND THE EYES
Unco and dowie – strange and low
Mid-lowsing time – midday mealtime

JUDGE NOT
Carle – man, fellow
Lug in – listen in

THE FIRE A MAN MAKES FOR HIMSELF
Sitig – midden, dung-heap
Crùisgean – cruisie, a basic lamp made with an open pan to burn oil
Glaur – mud, dirt

THE WOMAN IN THE STONES

Waulking – the process of working newly-woven tweed fabric by hand to shrink it, tightening the threads and increasing its strength and thickness (also called fulling)

NANNY

Grat – cried
Bogle – ghost
Wabbit – tired, worn out
Winnock bunker – windowsill

LITTLE YELLOW COMB

Lochlann – Norway or Scandinavia more generally
Geas – a magical obligation or prohibition; a magic spell

POINTING THE FINGER

Martinmas – the feast of St Martin of Tours on Friday 11 November. Historically communities celebrated the completion of the harvest, the end of autumn and the start of winter preparations on this day.

ACKNOWLEDGEMENTS

M Y FIRST THANKS must go to Rachel Newton and Lauren MacColl for asking me to take part in their wonderful project from which this book was born (more on page 201). They are both brilliant women and I count myself very lucky to call them friends. I also count myself lucky to have known Rachel's late mum; the poem in the dedication in her memory is by Sìleas na Ceapaich. Creative Scotland generously supported Rachel and Lauren and my own contribution to the project; thank you to all there.

The team at Black & White are always a joy to work with and I'm grateful to Ali and Campbell for letting me continue exploring the stories of Scottish women. Emma Hargrave kindly supported in developing the original structure, and Emma's successor Clem Flanagan has been the kindest of editors. Thomas Ross and Tonje Hefte have again made the book quite beautiful, and Helen Crawford White's cover brought tears to my eyes. Rachel Morrell kindly checked 'Doll' for its portrayal of eighteenth-century Jamaica. Thanks to you all.

Many people inspired the writing, helped with queries, read over drafts of the stories and listened to me ramble on (or in the case of my parents, all four: Dad, you can pick up the phone again safe in the knowledge I'm not ringing to ask which version of the Bible might have been in use in East Lothian in 1597 or what exactly a bailie did). My husband Tom Morgan-Jones supported me completely as he always does. Tom read everything in draft, as did my brilliant friend Viccy Adams. Dr Abigail Burnyeat sent me a news article about Katherine MacKinnon, whose ordeal took place in the village where Abi lives today, prompting Katherine's inclusion in the collection. Dr D. W. Stewart helped me in a quest to track down an elusive commentary on the Eachlair Ùrlair I was sure I'd read in the nineties … *somewhere in an article on … something else.* Geraldine Bradley let me think out loud over coffee and generously shared her own thoughts developed in years of psychology and Women's Studies work. Maurice Henderson kindly agreed to check Da Dim and shared with me his deep knowledge and love of Shetland and its history and traditions. Thanks to you all/ ceud mìle taing dhuibh uile.

Various work and writing commitments have meant I've been lucky enough to meet some of the brilliant folk working to help us better understand the history of witches in Scotland. At Creative Scotland I heard an electrifying reading by Dr Louise Yeoman of the papers from a case as part of a broader discussion of misogyny in Scotland, then and now. Through *Warriors and Witches and Damn Rebel Bitches* I got to speak with Claire Mitchell and Zoe Venditozzi, the powerhouse team behind Witches of Scotland. They and many others have inspired me and their work has informed me, and I thank them for that.

All errors are of course my own. My aim for the book was to place a stone on the cairn of the women featured within it. In a work blending fiction and non-fiction, and created at a significant distance of time, I am sure that I have erred in how I have depicted them. I hope they would forgive me. I am deeply sorry for what Scotland did to them.

MAIRI KIDD is a writer, publisher and translator and has worked for many years in literature and arts development, including a stint as Head of Literature at Creative Scotland. Her previous books include *Warriors and Witches and Damn Rebel Bitches: Scottish Women to Live Your Life By* and *Feisty & Fiery & Fierce: Badass Women to Live Your Life By from the Celtic Nations of Scotland, Ireland and Wales.* Mairi also writes for children, and has written for stage, screen and radio in Gaelic and English. Having first been inspired to write about Scotland's women when living in the original home of scandalous society beauty Rachel Chiesley, Lady Grange, Mairi has now forsaken seventeenth-century ghosts for a home by the sea in Portobello, where she lives with her husband and a very handsome black cat.